GERMAN COMME… …ER
VS
BRITISH CRUISER
The Atlantic & The Pacific 1941

ROBERT FORCZYK

First published in Great Britain in 2010 by Osprey Publishing,
PO Box 883, Oxford, OX1 9PL, UK
PO Box 3985, New York, NY 10185-3985, USA
Email: info@ospreypublishing.com

Osprey Publishing is part of the Osprey Group.

Transferred to digital print on demand 2014

First published 2010
2nd impression 2011

Printed and bound by PrintOnDemand-Worldwide.com,
Peterborough, UK

A CIP catalogue record for this book is available from the
British Library

ISBN: 978 1 84603 918 8
PDF ISBN: 978 1 84908 284 6
ePub ISBN: 978 1 78200 844 6

Page layout by Ken Vail Graphic Design, Cambridge, UK
Index by Alan Thatcher
Typeset in ITC Conduit and Adobe Garamond
Maps by Bounford.com
3D BEVs by Ian Palmer
Originated by PDQ Digital Media Solutions, Suffolk, UK

The Woodland Trust
Osprey Publishing are supporting the Woodland Trust, the
UK's leading woodland conservation charity, by funding the
dedication of trees.

www.ospreypublishing.com

Imperial War Museum Collections
Many of the photos in this book come from the Imperial War
Museum's huge collections which cover all aspects of conflict
involving Britain and the Commonwealth since the start of the
twentieth century. These rich resources are available online to
search, browse and buy at www.iwmcollections.org.uk. In
addition to Collections Online, you can visit the Visitor Rooms
where you can explore over 8 million photographs, thousands
of hours of moving images, the largest sound archive of its kind
in the world, thousands of diaries and letters written by people
in wartime, and a huge reference library. To make an
appointment, call (020) 7416 5320, or e-mail mail@iwm.org.uk.
Imperial War Museum www.iwm.org.uk

Acknowledgements

I would like to thank Commodore Bob Trotter, OAM RAN (ret'd),
director of the Finding Sydney Foundation, as well as the staffs
of the Bundesarchiv, the Australian War Memorial, the National
Archives and Records Administration (NARA) and the Imperial
War Museum (IWM) for their help in pulling together
photographs and other materials for this project.

Dedication
This volume is dedicated to 1st Lt David T. Wright II, 2-1 IN, 2nd
Infantry Division, KIA September 14, 2009, Helmand Province,
Afghanistan.

Editor's note
Technical specifications for British and German ships are given
in imperial and metric respectively, according to contemporary
national systems of measurement. The following chart provides
metric/imperial conversion factors:

1 mile = 1.6km

1lb = 0.45kg

1yd = 0.9m

1ft = 0.3m

1in = 2.54cm/25.4mm

1gal = 4.5 liters

1 ton (US) = 0.9 tonnes

CONTENTS

INTRODUCTION

"…in action with British cruiser. Fighting for the glory and honor of Germany. A last greeting to our relatives."
Last message from *Hilfskreuzer Leopard*, sunk March 16, 1917, by British cruiser HMS *Achilles*

At the beginning of the 20th century, it was no secret that Great Britain's center of gravity was its immense economic power, fueled by its control of nearly half the world's international shipping and trade. Consequently, Britain's greatest vulnerability was its merchant fleet, which consisted of more than 20,000 ships. In order to protect this shipping from potential adversaries, Britain used its wealth to create and maintain the world's most powerful navy. While Britain relied on its battle fleets based in home waters and the Mediterranean to contain direct threats to its naval dominance, the Royal Navy's numerous cruiser squadrons were the backbone of commerce protection overseas.

Imperial Germany also recognized the vulnerability of British maritime trade, and as early as 1895 began experimenting with converting suitable passenger liners into commerce raiders. The Kaiserliche Marine (Imperial Navy) believed that large, fast ocean liners would be ideal for conducting commerce raiding against Britain's distant shipping lanes, and they developed elaborate plans to convert a wide variety of civilian shipping into *Hilfskreuzer* (auxiliary cruisers) when the need arose. The sudden start of the war in August 1914, however, caught the Kaiserliche Marine flat-footed, and the only forces initially available for commerce raiding were Vizeadmiral Graf Maximilian von Spee's cruiser squadron in the Far East, the independent cruisers *Karlsruhe* in the Caribbean and *Königsberg* in German East Africa, and three large German passenger liners in the North Atlantic.

These German commerce raiders enjoyed a brief period of success in the opening months of the war, with *Karlsruhe* and *Emden* (detached from Spee's squadron) sinking 40 merchantmen totaling 142,000 tons in the Atlantic and Indian Ocean. Although two of the *Hilfskreuzer* were sunk by British cruisers before they were able to accomplish anything, the *Kronprinz Wilhelm* remained at sea for 251 days and destroyed 15 enemy ships. The Kaiserliche Marine was particularly successful in establishing at-sea replenishment of coal for the *Hilfskreuzer*, utilizing German merchant ships operating freely from neutral South American ports. Yet except for the *Kronprinz Wilhelm*, all the other German commerce raiders were neutralized by mid November 1914 and the Royal Navy believed that the threat of commerce raiding had been defeated. In fact, they had only experienced the opening round.

Failure taught the Kaiserliche Marine some valuable lessons about commerce raiding. In particular, it learned that range and endurance were more important for a raider than speed or firepower. Furthermore, using well-known passenger liners as *Hilfskreuzer* deprived these raiders of the advantages of anonymity and surprise. By mid 1915, the British blockade in the North Sea was too tight for any raider to fight its way through, and instead the Germans had to rely on guile and deception. A junior officer, Leutnant zur See Theodor Wolff, wrote a memorandum in August 1915 that suggested that converted freighters, with large coal-carrying capacity and hidden armament, would be ideally suited to commerce raiding. Two weeks later, Wolff's memorandum was sent to the *Admiralstab* (Admiralty Staff). His idea was accepted by the Kaiserliche Marine and became the blueprint for Germany's commerce raiding doctrine for the current war and the next one.

Based upon this concept, a nondescript freighter was out-fitted as a raider, albeit a disguised one, and went to sea on December 29, 1915, as the SMS *Möwe*. The first of

The protected cruiser HMS *Highflyer*, which was the victor on August 26, 1914, over the German *Kaiser Wilhelm der Grosse*, a passenger liner converted into a *Hilfskreuzer*. HMS *Highflyer* was typical of the coal-burning Royal Navy cruisers designed at the turn of the century for commerce protection. She only had patrolling endurance of 3½ days and an effective radius of action of 600 miles from a friendly port or collier, which greatly reduced her ability to protect the mercantile trade routes. (Author's Collection)

The *Hilfskreuzer* that set the mold for the commerce raiders of World War II: SMS *Wolf II* in 1917. On her 451-day patrol, *Wolf* cruised the Atlantic, Indian, and Pacific Oceans and captured or sank 120,000 tons of shipping before returning home in triumph. (Author's Collection)

the new breed of *Hilfskreuzer* easily passed through the British blockade around the Faroe Islands and then conducted three months of successful raiding in the South Atlantic. Although the British deployed more than a dozen cruisers to search for the raider, they came up empty-handed. Four more disguised raiders followed in 1916 and two of these raiders – the SMS *Möwe* and the SMS *Wolf* – succeeded in reaching the Atlantic and between them eliminated 74 vessels totaling 307,519 tons before returning to Germany in triumph. *Wolf*, which carried enough coal to cruise for 32,000 miles without refueling, even made it around the Cape of Good Hope and captured six ships in the Indian Ocean and five in the Pacific. Suddenly, the British Admiralty realized that the threat of commerce raiding was not restricted to the Atlantic.

In August 1914, the Royal Navy had 108 cruisers, but half were obsolescent and only a few dozen were actually suited for trade protection duties. Caught short-handed with insufficient cruisers, the Admiralty decided to convert a number of civilian vessels into Armed Merchant Cruisers (AMCs) to provide greater presence on Britain's sea-lanes. The Admiralty favored large, fast passenger liners for the AMC role and armed them with surplus 4.7in and 6in guns. Most of these vessels were formed into the 10th Cruiser Squadron and used to patrol the North Sea and the North Atlantic. In an era when there were few maritime patrol aircraft and many merchant ships lacked long-range radios to warn of attacks, the Royal Navy usually assigned its remaining cruisers to patrol near neutral ports or other anchorages where a raider could be expected to meet covertly with a collier. These tactics worked in 1914, but they failed utterly in 1916, since the new *Hilfskreuzer* operated with no logistical support network. Even when the British were able to find a raider, German disguises were so effective that their ships often succeeded in bluffing their way past cursory inspections. On Christmas Day 1916, the British AMC HMS *Avenger* stopped the disguised German raider *Seeadler* off the coast of Norway and sent a boarding party aboard, but the British sailors were fooled by the vessel and crew's detailed Norwegian disguise and allowed them to proceed.

When raiders were discovered, they proved quite dangerous. On the morning of February 29, 1916, the AMC HMS *Alcantara* encountered the German raider *Greif* – which was disguised as a Norwegian freighter – off the Shetland Islands. The *Alcantara* imprudently approached to within 2,000 yards to check the identity of this vessel when the *Greif* suddenly opened fire with its 15cm guns and hit the AMC with a torpedo. *Alcantara* was mortally wounded, but before sinking its 6in guns it managed to set the *Greif* afire, causing the Germans to abandon ship. The action between the *Alcantara* and the *Greif* was remarkably similar to the battle between HMAS *Sydney* and the *Kormoran* 25 years later and demonstrates the edge that disguised raiders had in the opening moments of combat.

Between 1914 and 1917, Imperial Germany converted a total of 16 *Hilfskreuzer*, of which 12 were operationally deployed as commerce raiders, and they succeeded in sinking or capturing more than 357,000 tons of Allied shipping. The Royal Navy

The 14,349-ton passenger liner *Kaiser Wilhelm der Grosse* proved to be a poor *Hilfskreuzer* due to limited endurance and her easy identifiability as a four-stack liner. In August 1914 she snuck into the neutral Spanish port of Rio de Oro in Africa to meet with three colliers, but was surprised by the British cruiser HMS *Highflyer*. After a 95-minute gunnery duel, the liner was scuttled, although the British claim that it was sunk by gunfire. This action became the model for how the Royal Navy thought it would deal with raiders that evaded the North Sea blockade. (Author's Collection)

managed to sink six raiders, four by regular cruisers and two by AMCs. Royal Navy cruiser patrols in the North Sea proved particularly adept, sinking three raiders trying to break through the blockade. Yet the British ability to hunt down disguised raiders once they got past the North Sea blockade was almost negligible, and the duel between British cruisers and *Hilfskreuzer* in World War I was at best a draw. Nevertheless, the Admiralty was satisfied that its methods were effective in dealing with enemy commerce raiding. Convoys, protected by sufficient cruisers, were seen as the answer to both U-boats and surface raiders. In response to the few raiders that managed to get past the blockade, the Royal Navy began to build larger, faster cruisers that were specifically designed for overseas commerce protection.

Each side learned different lessons from World War I. The Germans learned that the most important characteristics of a *Hilfskreuzer* was its ability to pass convincingly as a neutral or friendly merchant vessel and, as already noted, to have the endurance to operate far from home without regular logistical support. The Royal Navy believed that AMCs were adequate against raiders and that the best means to defeat raiders was to construct an air-tight blockade in the North Sea. If any raiders made it past the blockade, the Royal Navy's overseas cruiser squadrons would handle them. However, the British put little effort into establishing a system to confirm quickly the identity of merchant ships when spotted by patrolling cruisers, in order to deprive German

The brand-new *Kent*-class heavy cruiser HMS *Cornwall* on the China Station in 1929. *Cornwall* was a typical "Treaty Cruiser," and spent most of her career on foreign stations. She was flagship of the 5th Cruiser Squadron in Singapore at the start of World War II and was involved in anti-raider operations in the South Atlantic and Indian Ocean throughout 1939–42. (IWM, FL 8535)

Hilfskreuzer of their main advantage – anonymity. Nor did the Royal Navy understand that speed and firepower were less important for their cruiser squadrons to defeat the *Hilfskreuzer* than endurance and at-sea replenishment.

Based upon its World War I experience, the inter-war Admiralty believed that it needed a minimum of 70 cruisers just for the trade protection mission. When war broke out in September 1939, however, the Royal Navy only had a total of 58 cruisers in service. Eighteen of these vessels were heavy cruisers, while the rest were 6in gun light cruisers. Unlike World War I, the Admiralty moved expeditiously to establish convoys, which began in mid September 1939. When the German pocket battleship *Admiral Graf Spee* began operating in the South Atlantic in October 1939, the Admiralty did not hesitate to send three powerful hunting groups to search for it, and in December the German warship was intercepted by British cruisers off Montevideo and forced to scuttle after the battle of the River Plate. The search for the *Graf Spee* reinforced the Admiralty's belief that the main threat from German commerce raiding would come from regular warships, rather than disguised raiders. By the summer of 1940, Britain had its convoy system in place and the Admiralty was confident that it had enough cruisers and the correct tactics to counter any German commerce raiding efforts. This assumption proved to be sadly wrong.

On the other side of the hill, the outbreak of war with Great Britain came as a great shock to the German Seekriegsleitung (SKL; Sea Warfare Command) in Berlin. The Oberkommando der Marine (OKM; Naval High Command) had hoped to build up a balanced fleet, but when war came suddenly in September 1939 the only viable naval strategy was commerce raiding. Yet there were only two operational pocket battleships and 23 U-boats available for long-range anti-commerce operations. Faced with this reality, the SKL activated its plans to unleash a new force of *Hilfskreuzer* upon the world's oceans to savage British trade. Instead of deploying only one commerce raider at a time as in World War I, this time the SKL wanted to begin with six *Hilfskreuzer* sailing nearly simultaneously, followed by six more within months. Seven were able to sail in 1940, with more being converted for future patrols.

Unlike a standard cruiser vs. cruiser duel, where firepower, maneuverability and armored protection would decide the outcome, the duel between German *Hilfskreuzer* and British cruisers was more often decided by cunning and intelligence, rather than superior technical capabilities. The first part of the duel consisted of a cat-and-mouse chase that spanned a huge expanse of water, stretching from the South Atlantic across the Indian Ocean to the Pacific, and conducted when shipborne radars were uncommon. The Germans used their ability to alter the appearance of their *Hilfskreuzer* to evade detection, sometimes literally passing under the noses of searching British cruisers. The British, however, eventually gained an advantage through signals intelligence, which would enable them to target the vital clandestine naval supply network that the SKL had established to support its overseas raiders. Yet even when the Royal Navy could determine approximately where a *Hilfskreuzer* was operating, it was no mean feat to actually run one to ground. Victory in the 'duel' was determined by tactical execution, which required positively identifying a commerce raider and successfully attacking it, before the raider decided to drop its disguise and fight.

CHRONOLOGY

1895

The Kaiserliche Marine experiments with converting a civilian steamer into a *Hilfskreuzer*

1912

The Admiralty proposes an 8,000-ton 'Atlantic Cruiser' for trade-protection against German commerce raiders, but the idea is shelved

1914

August   The Kaiserliche Marine begins *Hilfskreuzer* operations in the Atlantic

1915

August 15   Leutnant zur See Theodor Wolff writes memo on disguised *Hilfskreuzer*

November 1   The freighter *Pungo* is commissioned as the *Hilfskreuzer* SMS *Möwe*

1916

February 29   SMS *Greif* is sunk off Norway – the first disguised German *Hilfskreuzer* to be sunk by a British cruiser

June 3   First British *Hawkins*-class cruiser laid down; it is designed for long-range trade-protection

1928

May 10   HMS *Cornwall* commissioned

1929

May 18   HMS *Devonshire* commissioned

1935

September 24   HMAS *Sydney* commissioned

1938

Kormoran and *Thor* are completed

The freighter *Kurmark* before the war. The German SKL identified this vessel as a good candidate for conversion to *Hilfskreuzer* in the event of war and it would eventually enter Kriegsmarine service as the *Orion*. (Author's Collection)

1939

August 23	The British begin converting AMCs
September 3	The German SKL begins converting its first three *Hilfskreuzer*
November 30	*Atlantis* commissioned in the Kriegsmarine (German Navy)
December 9	*Orion*, *Widder*, *Pinguin*, and *Komet* commissioned in the Kriegsmarine

1940

March 11	*Atlantis* sails, the first *Hilfskreuzer* to deploy
March 15	*Thor* commissioned in the Kriegsmarine
April 6	*Orion* sails
May 6	*Widder* sails
June 6	*Thor* sails
June 15	*Pinguin* sails
July 3	*Komet* sails
July 18	Survivors from one of *Widder*'s victims provide Admiralty with first accurate description of a *Hilfskreuzer*

October 9	*Kormoran* commissioned in the Kriegsmarine
December 3	*Kormoran* sails
December	Admiralty introduces secret call sign for each merchant ship, in order to counter *Hilfskreuzer* false-flag tactics

1941

January 23	Admiralty issues CAFO 143 on "Raider Identification"
April 9	*Thor* sinks HMS *Voltaire*
May 8	*Pinguin* sunk by HMS *Cornwall*
November 19	*Kormoran* and HMAS *Sydney* both sunk in battle off Australian coast
November 22	*Atlantis* sunk by HMS *Devonshire*

HMS *Cardiff*, a C-class cruiser commissioned in June 1917. The C-Class set the standard for future British cruiser development by eliminating the previous mix of 6in and 4in guns in favor of a uniform armament of 6in guns positioned on the centerline. HMS *Cardiff* was pressed into duty with the Northern Patrol in 1939 to guard the GIUK Gap, but her limited patrol endurance of only five–seven days proved unsatisfactory. (IWM, Q 65725)

DESIGN AND DEVELOPMENT

BRITISH

Throughout the 19th century, the Royal Navy viewed trade protection as one of its foremost missions and it sought to develop warships best suited for this task. The term "cruiser" evolved in the 1870s as various types of British frigates and corvettes gradually coalesced into a new class of medium-size warship designed for long-range patrolling. In 1880, the first modern, all-steel cruisers – the *Leander*-class with 6in guns – were laid down in Scottish yards. These cruisers cost £200,000 each and had the primary mission of trade protection. Within five years, two emerging technologies – the triple expansion (TE) engine and quick-firing (QF) guns – began to influence cruiser development. TE engines provided coal-fired warships with sufficient range for long-endurance "cruising" and QF guns allowed smaller warships to achieve a satisfactory rate of fire to overwhelm enemy commerce raiders. By 1889, both innovations were put into the *Apollo*-class cruisers, which were capable of conducting a 30-day patrol. Given their modest cost of about £300,000 each, the Royal Navy could afford to build large quantities of these new 6in gun cruisers for trade protection.

The British Admiralty, however, made a fundamental strategic error with the Naval Defence Act of 1889 by dividing cruisers up into three new categories. First-class cruisers were virtually small battleships, ranging in size from 7,000 to 14,000 tons and armed with 9.2in and 6in guns, while the other two classes were in the 3,000–5,000-ton range and armed with 6in and 4.7in guns. Trade protection was still the primary mission of the Second-class cruisers, but the First-class cruisers were expected to operate with the main battle fleets, while the Third-class cruisers acted as scouts.

HMS *Effingham* of the *Hawkins*-class in 1930. The *Hawkins*-class set the standard for British heavy cruisers and were designed for trade defense against German commerce raiders. This class had an endurance of up to 16 days at cruising speeds and were good sea boats, but they lacked a floatplane. (IWM, Q 65717)

A few years later, the French commissioned the armored cruiser *Dupuy de Lôme*, and then the Russians built the armored cruiser *Rurik*, both intended for long-range commerce raiding operations. Instead of taking time to evaluate the actual threat posed by these foreign ships, the Admiralty hastily decided that the best way to counter them was to build larger and faster cruisers of its own. Two *Powerful*-class cruisers were built for £750,000 each in 1895, and instead of building a balanced cruiser force the Admiralty developed a preference for larger and more expensive cruisers. Construction of the cheaper, workhorse Second-class cruisers soon came to a virtual halt in favor of bigger vessels. While large cruisers had the speed and firepower to defeat enemy cruisers, they tended to be coal-burning fuel hogs that were poorly suited to trade defense. The Admiralty was also reluctant to send these expensive First-class cruisers to overseas stations, and preferred to keep them in home waters. Somewhere along the way, the requirements for trade protection got lost in the rush to build bigger cruisers and members of the Admiralty even began to question whether the mission was still feasible. Thus, in over-reacting to a hypothetical threat, the Royal Navy gradually transformed its cruisers into a force that was poorly suited to accomplishing one of its core missions.

The Admiralty really lost its sense of strategic priorities in 1904, when Jackie Fisher became First Sea Lord. Fisher was mesmerized by size, speed, and firepower, and he accelerated the trend toward larger cruisers. Not only did Fisher authorize the 14,600-ton *Minotaur*-class at a cost of over £1.4 million each, but he embarked on a quest to develop the *Invincible*-class battlecruisers in 1906. In Fisher's mind, battleships and cruisers were morphing into a new type of warship and he allowed technology rather than strategic priorities and doctrine to drive cruiser development. Believing that flimsy Second-class cruisers, now redesignated "protected cruisers," were "too small to fight and too slow to run away" from enemy commerce raiders, Fisher declared that battlecruisers would henceforth protect British trade. To Fisher's credit, however, within a few years he realized that there would never be enough expensive armored cruisers or battlecruisers for trade defense and he authorized work to begin again on developing light cruisers with the *Town*-class in 1909. A total of 21 units of this class, reasonably priced at £350,000 each, were built and they would play a major role in commerce protection in the coming war. Fisher also pushed the introduction of oil-fueled cruisers over coal, which would gradually extend the endurance of the newer ships to two weeks, at economical speeds.

When war came in 1914, early battle experience against German commerce raiders appeared to bear out Fisher's policies, when the *Town*-class cruiser HMAS *Sydney* used its superior speed and firepower to defeat the SMS *Emden* at the battle of Cocos in November 1914. A month later, the battlecruisers HMS *Invincible* and *Inflexible* and three armored cruisers were able to outrun and outfight von Spee's squadron at the battle of the Falkland Islands. This engagement was the kind of duel that the Admiralty expected to fight against commerce raiders, with superior speed and firepower defeating an enemy flying its national flag, in a fair fight.

Yet it was soon apparent that both armored cruisers and battlecruisers were vulnerable to other forms of enemy attack, and their period of ascendency in Admiralty thinking came to a halt when three of each were blown to pieces at the battle of Jutland in 1916. After Jutland, the Admiralty came to realize that fleet actions were infrequent and that it was better to have many lightly armed cruisers rather than a few heavily armed cruisers.

By mid war, trade protection was the priority as U-boat attacks increased and the first of the disguised *Hilfskreuzer* began to appear in the Atlantic. Sir Eustace Tennyson-d'Eyncourt, Director of Naval Construction (DNC) for the Admiralty, designed a series of improved light cruisers, beginning with the *Ceres*-class, followed by the *Capetown*- and *Danae*-classes in 1918. Unlike earlier light cruisers that had a confusing mix of 6in and 4in guns, these late-war light cruisers carried a standardized armament of five or six 6in guns. In response to the success of German commerce raiders, Tennyson-d'Eyncourt also designed the 9,750-ton *Cavendish*-class, armed with 7.5in guns and better endurance than the previous armored cruisers. All four of these classes were still under construction when the Armistice occurred, and they would strongly influence the next generation of British cruisers.

In the immediate aftermath of the war, the Royal Navy completed the last seven of the C-, D-, and *Emerald*-class light cruisers by 1921. Just as the Admiralty was beginning to consider the next generation of cruisers, representatives of the major naval powers met in Washington to negotiate a treaty to prevent a new naval arms race. The resultant Washington Naval Treaty, signed on February 6, 1922, influenced cruiser design by limiting tonnage to no more than 10,000 tons per ship (Article XI) and armament to no more than 8in guns (Article XII). Although the Admiralty viewed the Washington Naval Treaty as inimical to warship development, it actually benefited the Royal Navy by cancelling the new G-3 battlecruisers and a host of other white elephant projects. Far from harming the Royal Navy's core mission of protecting trade, the treaties forced the Admiralty to concentrate on building greater numbers of medium-sized cruisers that were better suited for trade defense. The Washington Treaty also forced the Royal Navy to discard almost all of its remaining battlecruisers and armored cruisers.

Britain, France, the United States, Italy, and Japan all began building "Treaty Cruisers" that met the new restrictions. Since all the armored cruisers were discarded and the Royal Navy only had a single large cruiser in service at the time of the treaty's

SCHIFF 41, HSK 8, *KORMORAN*

Built	1938
Commissioned	Kriegsmarine: October 9, 1940
Displacement	19,900 tons (standard)
Dimensions	538ft (overall); beam 66ft 3in, draft 27ft 10in
Engines	4 9-cyl diesels, plus 2 electric motors
Maximum speed	18 knots
Endurance	84,500 miles at 10 knots (352 days)
Armament	6x 15cm/45 guns in single mounts; 1x 75mm; 4x 37mm; 5x 20mm single mounts; 6x 21in torpedo tubes; 360 mines; 2 Arado 196A-1 floatplanes.
Crew	400

signature, the Admiralty decided to focus on designing a new generation of 8in gun cruisers for trade protection. Once again, the Admiralty saw superior firepower as the solution to commerce raiding. However, the Royal Navy had no existing 8in guns in service, so it had to design a new weapon. Work began on the Mark VIII L/50 gun in 1923. It took four years to bring it into service, but even then the weapon was plagued with defects. The Admiralty began building seven Kent-class heavy cruisers at a cost of about £1.97 million each. These cruisers were built just under the 10,000-ton limit and each carried four twin 8in gun turrets, which left little space for armored protection. Instead, Tennyson-d'Eyncourt utilized a box protection scheme of 4in thick armor around each of the four turret barbettes and magazines, but the rest of the hull was protected by little more than 1in thick plating. While this lack of protection made the Kent-class cruisers poorly suited for a fleet role, they were well suited to the commerce protection role due to their excellent habitability for their crews and their long endurance. In an era when refueling at sea was virtually unknown, the Royal Navy wanted a cruiser that could patrol the wide expanses of the South Atlantic and Indian Ocean for several weeks without having to return to a base to refuel.

All seven Kent-class cruisers were commissioned in 1928, but even before they were in service the Royal Navy began constructing four ships of the modified London-class and two of the Norfolk-class. Collectively, these three classes were known as the County-class and all 13 were in commission by 1930. The County-class cruisers suffered from inadequacies, however, beginning with the troublesome new 8in Mark VIII gun. When HMS Devonshire went to its firing trials on July 26, 1929, an explosion caused by a catastrophic breech failure in X-turret killed 18 crewmembers. The 8in guns also suffered from a low rate of fire, which forced the British to spend considerable effort modifying the turrets. Yet firing trials in 1929 also indicated that the 8in gun was very accurate, straddling the target in 40 percent of 15 salvoes fired at ranges of 12,000–24,000 yards.

Improved gunnery accuracy became a Holy Grail for the Royal Navy after the losses suffered at Jutland, and the Admiralty intended to provide its new cruisers with the very latest in fire control. In 1926 a Director Control Tower (DCT) was mounted on the cruiser HMS Enterprise and employed a 15ft rangefinder, gyro-stabilized telescopes, and a rudimentary computer device to provide accurate shooting solutions out to 33,000 yds. Early experiments validated the DCT concept but it was too late for most of the County-class ships and was only installed on the last two, HMS Norfolk and Devonshire. The Royal Navy began using DCT-equipped cruisers in trials during the 1930s to put salvoes accurately on target using a "ladder" system of quickly adjusting rounds onto target, which would give British cruisers a decided advantage in long-range actions.

Apart from improved gunnery, the Admiralty was keen to add catapults to its cruisers, so they could carry reconnaissance floatplanes, and to improve armored protection, but the new cruisers were so close to the treaty limit that other items would have to be removed. The DNC opted to remove the torpedo tubes from the County-class cruiser, cut down the rear deck, and make other extensive modifications in order to accommodate a catapult and aircraft hangar for up to three floatplanes. A narrow,

4in-thick armored belt was also added at the waterline. In order to develop a heavy cruiser with more room for new equipment, the Royal Navy decided to build two ships of the smaller *York*-class. The new DNC, Sir William J. Berry, omitted the fourth 8in gun turret, which made these cruisers 55ft shorter and 1,600 tons lighter, thereby allowing more space for armored protection. Significantly, the *York*-class cruisers had about double the fuel efficiency of the larger *County*-class, improving their suitability for commerce protection.

Yet just as British naval designers were learning to build effective cruisers within the limits of the Washington Naval Treaty, the ground shifted under their feet again when Britain signed the London Naval Treaty on April 22, 1930. The new treaty distinguished between 8in gun heavy cruisers and 6in gun light cruisers and set restrictive limits for both types. Under the treaty's Article 15, the Royal Navy was limited to only 146,800 tons of heavy cruisers, which meant that no new 8in gun cruisers could be built until the *Kent*-class was due for replacement. However, Article 20 left the Royal Navy the option to build up to 91,000 tons of 6in gun cruisers by 1936 in order to replace the older C-class cruisers, so the Admiralty shifted to a new phase of light cruiser development. Design work began on the 6in/50 Mark XXIII gun to equip the new generation of light cruisers.

Sir Arthur Johns, who took over the DNC from 1930 to 1936, was responsible for designing most of this next generation of British light cruisers. Construction of the five ships of the *Leander*-class began in June 1931, followed by the three ships of the *Perth*-class in August 1933 and all eight were in commission by mid 1936. These cruisers were in the 7,200-ton range, carried four twin 6in gun turrets and had decent cruising range. However, each light cruiser cost £1.5 million, which was not much less than a *Kent*-class heavy cruiser. Since Britain's defense spending was already constricted by the global Depression, the Admiralty sought a smaller and more economical variant when it ordered the four ships of the *Arethusa*-class in 1932.

Once German rearmament became obvious and both the Americans and Japanese began building larger cruisers, the Royal Navy lost interest in honoring treaty restrictions and began building a new group of heavily armed and better-protected light cruisers. Work began on five *Southampton*-class light cruisers in 1934, each of which carried four triple 6in gun turrets on a 9,100-ton hull. These cruisers were nearly as large as the *County*-class ships, but more maneuverable and better protected. Three slightly larger models appeared as the *Gloucester*-class in 1936. When the restrictions of the London Naval Treaty expired in December 1936, the Admiralty authorized two 11,580-ton cruisers of the *Edinburgh*-class, armed with four triple 6in gun turrets. Although the DNC had been

On June 12, 1941, the *Southampton*-class light cruiser HMS *Sheffield* intercepted the German resupply tanker *Friederich Breme* off Cape Finisterre as a result of the Y-Service decoding the German *Heimisch* cipher. Empty cardboard cordite cases lie around the two forward 6in Mark XXII twin turrets after the short engagement. The new 6in gun enjoyed a significant advantage in range over the 15cm guns used by the German *Hilfskreuzer*. (IWM, A 4401)

BRITISH CRUISER DIRECTOR CONTROL TOWER (DCT)

Plot room

Transmitting station

The main battery on British cruisers is directed and fired from a Director Sight mounted in the Director Control Tower (DCT), which is situated in the after end of the bridge. The target is initially acquired by lookouts using optical sights on the bridge, which relay its bearing to the DCT, which is then turned to face the target. The DCT crew operates a stabilized telescope and a pair of stereoscopic binoculars, which they use to determine the target's range, speed, and bearing. This information is then sent by telephone to the transmitting station below deck and the plot room. In the transmitting station, the team uses the Admiralty Fire Control Clock, a rudimentary computer-like device, to solve the fire control problem and to send the correct elevation and deflection solutions to the gun turrets. The gunnery officer in the DCT supervises this process and when DIRECTOR-firing mode is used, his team can fire all the turrets simultaneously from the DCT by means of a trigger or foot pedal. Once the rounds are on the way, the DCT determines the accuracy of the salvo and sends further corrections to bring the next salvo onto the target.

progressively adding minor armor upgrades on each new class of cruiser built since 1930, the end of treaty limitations enabled British designers to abandon the inferior box protection scheme and emplace a 4.8in thick armor belt on the *Edinburgh*-class. These ships were expensive at about £2.1 million each and lacked the range of the earlier *Kent*-class, but were better suited for a wider variety of missions. Subsequently, the DNC developed the 8,000-ton *Fiji*-class, armed with three triple 6in gun turrets, as a more economical variant, and the Admiralty ordered five in 1937–39. By 1939, the British cruiser force was divided into three main groupings: the elderly light cruisers and the *Hawkins*-class heavy cruisers of World War I origin, the 8in heavy gun cruisers built in the 1920s, and the modern 6in gun cruisers built in the 1930s.

Despite the lackluster performance of AMCs in World War I, the Admiralty enthusiastically endorsed their re-adoption by authorizing the conversion of 51 British, 2 Australian, and 1 New Zealand civilian ships on August 23, 1939. Once again, the Admiralty preferred fast passenger liners as AMCs and armed them with virtually the same weapons as in the last war, typically six–eight obsolete 6in guns and a couple of 12-pdr anti-aircraft (AA) guns. These ersatz cruisers were intended entirely for the commerce protection role, particularly on distant stations far removed from the main theater of war. Unfortunately for the AMC crews, there were few quiet areas in the coming conflict. The Admiralty realized that AMCs were poorly suited to a stand-up fight, but expected them to engage a *Hilfskreuzer* long enough for reinforcements to arrive.

Although intended for trade protection, British cruisers overseas tended to be tied to operating around bases such as Bermuda, Freetown, Colombo and Singapore due to the Royal Navy's slowness in perfecting replenishment at sea techniques. While the Royal Fleet Auxiliary had 14 fleet tankers at the start of the war, at-sea refueling was rarely conducted until late in the war, and cruisers in 1940–41 usually went to the nearest port for refueling. This doctrinal limitation helped to make British cruiser patrolling patterns more predictable and easier for German raiders to evade – a subtle defect that had significant implications for the cruiser versus *Hilfskreuzer* duel in 1940–41. During

GERMAN 15CM GUNSIGHT

The main armament on the Hilfskreuzer – the 15cm/45 SK L/45 C06 guns in single mounts – relied upon stereoscopic rangefinders to obtain the correct distance to the target. Compared to the coincidence rangefinders in use on most British cruisers, the German stereoscopic devices were better suited to quickly determining the range to targets under 10,000 yards. The gunnery officer would lay the yellow dot atop the center triangle on the sight reticule on a prominent object on the target, such as the funnel on a British cruiser.

this period, in technological terms the Royal Navy was also slow to adopt shipboard radar, and the handful of cruisers equipped with rudimentary surface search radars were usually kept with the Home Fleet. Aside from on-board floatplanes, the British cruisers of 1940–41 would have search capabilities little improved from the last war.

GERMAN

The Germany Navy had not forgotten the success of commerce raiders in World War I and Konteradmiral Karl August Nerger, former captain of the *Hilfskreuzer Wolf,* was still on the naval staff in the early 1930s. In May 1936, the SKL asked Nerger to compile a report on the lessons learned from commerce raiders during the war. Nerger's report, also drawing upon Count Nikolaus Dohna's experience on the *Möwe,* pointed out how a raider such as *Wolf* had been able to operate at sea for 451 days without any logistical support from home, and how a floatplane was vital for extending the search capabilities of the raider. Dohna's input emphasized the importance of the raider having a mine-laying capability, since one of *Möwe's* covertly laid mines had sunk the British pre-dreadnought HMS *King Edward VII* on January 6, 1916 – an impressive example of what would today be called "asymmetric warfare."

Using Nerger's report as a guide, the Kriegsmarine began providing covert subsidies to the Hansa and Fels commercial shipping lines to prepare some of their merchantmen to be used as commerce raiders in wartime. By January 1938, the OKM was serious enough about commerce raiding that it was including provisions for outfitting six *Hilfskreuzer* in its *Mobilmachungsplan Marine* (Naval Mobilization Plan), and it was during the subsequent Munich Crisis that specific ships and crews were designated. When war began in September 1939, the SKL activated the plan to equip these first six *Hilfskreuzer.* Two vessels from the Hamburg–Amerika Line, the *Kurmark* and the *Neumark,* and the *Goldenfels* from the Hansa Line, were immediately taken over for conversion.

The Kriegsmarine did not want a standard design for a *Hilfskreuzer,* since that would be inimical to establishing each raider's unique disguise. Indeed, medium-size freighters that appeared nondescript and commonplace on the world's seaways were preferred to larger or one-of-a-kind vessels that were easy to identify. Unlike the Royal Navy, the SKL rejected the idea of using large, fast passenger liners as naval auxiliaries. Heeding Nerger's study, the basic template that the SKL followed was to incorporate the essential characteristics of the successful SMS *Wolf* of 1917; a medium-sized freighter armed with six 15cm guns, torpedoes, mines, and a seaplane. the vessels that the SKL selected, however, ranged in size from a 3,287-ton banana boat to an 8,736-ton freighter, and this time the raiders were oil-fueled rather than coal-powered.

Conversion began almost immediately on the first three *Hilfskreuzer* in September 1939 at the DeSchiMAG yard in Bremen. Each vessel was given a cover identity that explained why a commercial vessel was being transformed into a naval auxiliary, as the

SKL did not want dockyard workers and various loose-lipped bureaucrats in port to know the true purpose of these ships. For example, the *Goldenfels*, which would become HSK-2 or the *Atlantis*, was described as a "depot ship." Since many naval offices involved in the conversion process were not appraised of the *Hilfskreuzer* project, the need for security created difficulties in obtaining items such as weaponry, aircraft, and other warlike equipment for a vessel that was ostensibly a support ship. Thus the *Hilfskreuzer* were in effect, in disguise even in their home ports. There was also resistance from more hidebound parts of the Kriegsmarine, which were reluctant to give scarce resources to what were regarded by some as "suicide ships." This situation was particularly true in regard to the acquisition of floatplanes for the *Hilfskreuzer*. Rather than getting the better Arado 196A-1 that were reserved for regular surface raiders, the inferior He-114C-2 was pawned off on the first batch of *Hilfskreuzer*.

One essential requirement for each *Hilfskreuzer* was that it had to have adequate internal space to store the supplies needed to sustain a man-of-war at sea for at least one year. Converting the *Goldenfels* to the *Atlantis* required doubling its internal fuel capacity and tripling its water capacity. Unlike civilian freighters that only spent a few weeks at sea, the *Hilfskreuzer* were designed to operate at least one year away from port, which required them to be much more self-reliant than standard warships. Adequate space also had to be made for a crew of up to 400 sailors as well as 200 or more prisoners, instead of the normal 40-man civilian crew.

As much as possible, the ships were supposed to retain their civilian appearance, but concealed weapons stations were built to give them the firepower roughly equivalent to that of a World War I light cruiser. Emplacing these weapons stations was difficult, since they had to have adequate traverse and fields of fire, but they also had to blend into a cluttered deck when not in use. Since there was not a great deal of surplus naval artillery lying around in German ports at the start of the war, the *Hilfskreuzer* were typically given older weapons that were stripped from obsolete warships. Their main armament would be the 15-cm SK L/45, which had entered service in 1908 and continued in limited production until about 1923. Contrary to what some sources have stated, the main armament for the *Hilfskreuzer* was not obsolete "forty-year old weapons," as claimed in some accounts, even though a number of the 15cm SK L/45 cannons were taken from the pre-dreadnoughts *Schleswig-Holstein* and *Schlesien* during the fitting-out process in late 1939. In point of fact, the two pre-dreadnoughts were only re-equipped with the 15cm guns in 1922 and even if every one of their 20 15cm guns were taken, this amount was still insufficient to provide the 42 15cm guns needed for the first seven *Hilfskreuzer*. Rather, it appears that many of the 15cm guns came from armament left over from the dreadnoughts and light cruisers under construction at the end of World War I, although *Kormoran* did carry one 15cm gun taken from

The freighter *Steiermark* under conversion to a *Hilfskreuzer* at Kiel during the fall of 1940. This vessel would enter Kriegsmarine service as the *Kormoran*. (Author's Collection)

HMAS *SYDNEY*

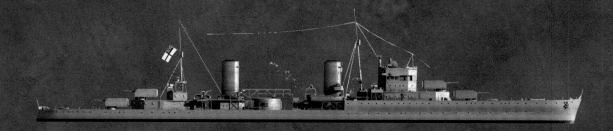

Built	19333—1935
Cost	1.5 million (approx)
Commissioned	RAN: September 24, 1935
Displacement	7,105 tons (srandard)
Dimensions	length 562ft 3in (overall); beam 56ft 8in, draft 19ft
Engines	4 geared engines
Maximum speed	31.5 knots
Endurance	7,000 miles at 16 knots (18 days)
Armament	8x 6in/50 Mk XXIII in twin turrets; 4x 4in/45 QF Mk V HA guns in single mounts; 8x 21in torpedo tubes; 1 Walrus floatplane.
Crew	645

the battlecruiser *Seydlitz*. Thus, the main armament on the *Hilfskreuzer* was not the most modern weapons available, but they were hardly antiques.

Far more serious was the issue of aged engine machinery, which was to plague several of the raiders. The sisterships *Kurmark* and *Neumark*, built in 1929–30, had received engines previously used in two other passenger liners, and both their powerplants proved to be seriously unreliable in service. Nevertheless, the SKL was eager to get commerce raiders to sea and was willing to overlook these technical defects.

Outfitting the first three raiders took about 90 days. The ex-*Goldenfels* was commissioned as the *Atlantis* (HSK-2) on November 30, 1939, followed by the ex-*Kurmark* as the *Orion* (HSK-1) and ex-*Neumark* as the *Widder* (HSK-3) on December 9. These three ships then did a couple weeks of work-up training in the Baltic and then gave most of their crews Christmas leave before their expected one-year deployments. DeSchiMAG then started work on converting the next three raiders. The SKL realized that the first raiders were far from perfect, but hoped to provide later *Hilfskreuzer* with modern weapons and more reliable engines.

Even if the raiders succeeded in capturing the fuel and food from Allied ships that they needed to sustain themselves for a one-year mission, the SKL knew that the *Hilfskreuzer* would still require some logistical support to resupply with ammunition and remove excess prisoners. A covert network of supply ships was developed, using blockade-runners from German-controlled ports and German civilian vessels interned in neutral ports. To make this system work, however, the *Hilfskreuzer* would have to communicate, and the SKL knew from British Radio Direction Finding (RDF) successes in World War I that this was potentially the commerce raider's greatest vulnerability. Thus, the Kriegsmarine went to great efforts to ensure that the raiders had the best possible secure communications. In addition to using an additional rotor on their Enigma encoding machines – unlike the more vulnerable Luftwaffe Enigma – the Kriegsmarine had developed extremely short brevity codes for their raiders that limited radio transmissions to only a few seconds.

Original name	Raider name	Raider designation	Launched	Tonnage	Owner/ Operator
Kurmark	*Orion*	HSK-1	1930	7,021	HAPAG
Goldenfels	*Atlantis*	HSK-2	1937	7,862	Hansa Line
Neumark	*Widder*	HSK-3	1930	7,851	HAPAG
Santa Cruz	*Thor*	HSK-4	1938	3,862	OPDR Line
Kandelfels	*Pinguin*	HSK-5	1936	7,766	Hansa Line
Ems	*Komet*	HSK-7	1937	3,287	NDL
Steiermark	*Kormoran*	HSK-8	1938	8,736	HAPAG

TECHNICAL SPECIFICATIONS

BRITISH

In combating the *Hilfskreuzer* threat, British cruisers relied on four key capabilities: their ability to communicate with shore-based command, their patrol endurance, their search radius, and their firepower. If a cruiser could spot a commerce raider, its superior speed and firepower gave it a decided advantage in any naval engagement, but finding the raider proved exceedingly difficult.

Unlike the days of sail, when a British frigate could independently patrol the seas and hope for a chance encounter with an enemy warship, by 1940 the Royal Navy's cruisers were heavily dependent upon maintaining communication with shore-based naval staffs for operational intelligence and logistical support. Naval staffs relayed RRR signals from merchant shipping under attack, which allowed cruisers to steam toward areas where raiders were known to be active. (The Admiralty mandated that all ships immediately send a QQQ radio signal upon sighting suspicious vessels and if fired upon, to send an RRR signal.) Hunting a raider also required radio coordination with other cruisers and shore-based aircraft. However, the Admiralty routinely ordered captains to employ radio silence while on patrol and only to report at the moment of contact with the enemy, since excessive radio traffic could alert a raider to the presence of nearby British cruisers. This over-caution created a dangerous Catch-22 situation, since the best way for cruiser captains to ascertain the true identity of suspicious merchant ships was to use the radio to contact regional naval headquarters, but normal procedures said this could compromise the cruiser's ability to surprise a raider. Thus, British commanders were often unwilling to use their radios, which was potentially their most effective weapon against the *Hilfskreuzer*. Furthermore, British cruisers in 1940 were typically equipped with a Type 36 or Type 48 medium-frequency transmitter, with an effective range of about 1,000 miles. If a cruiser operated further than this from its base, it sacrificed its ability to gather operational intelligence and became essentially "un-plugged" from external support.

Although British cruisers were capable of maximum speeds beyond what the *Hilfskreuzer* were capable of doing, this advantage rarely proved relevant. Rather, the cruiser's ability to hunt down commerce raiders depended far more on their capacity to remain at sea patrolling for as long as possible, before having to return to port to refuel. Common sense dictated that best endurance came from patrolling at speeds of 12–14 knots, although some captains preferred charging around the Indian Ocean like hounds after a fox. All the post-1921 British cruisers had a patrol endurance of up to 30 days with strict fuel economy, but the smaller cruisers such as the *Arethusa* and *Leander* classes, as well as the World War I-vintage cruisers, could only remain at sea for two weeks. When cruisers moved at speeds up to 30 knots, their endurance dropped precipitously. Normally, British cruisers conducting anti-raider patrols only cruised for about ten days before returning to base to refuel. The result of these restrictions on endurance and the British slowness in adopting refueling at sea meant that cruisers typically remained within about 500–600 miles of a friendly port. Furthermore, constant patrolling put great wear and tear on the engines and boilers of warships whether or not they found anything and British cruisers involved in commerce protection were often steaming over 60,000 miles a year in 1940–41. Under these conditions, mechanical reliability became an operational consideration and commanders became reluctant to push their handful of cruisers

The main radio room aboard the cruiser HMS *Shropshire*. One of the best weapons that British cruisers had against the *Hilfskreuzer* was their radios, which gave them the means to verify the identities of suspicious vessels. Unfortunately, the British obsession with radio silence while on patrol often undermined the effectiveness of this capability. (IWM, A 7599)

An RAF Short S. 19 Singapore flying boat, flown by 205 Squadron in the Far East and Indian Ocean until October 1941. In an effort to locate the *Komet* and *Orion*, four Singapores were loaned to the RNZAF's No. 5 Squadron operating in Fiji. The Singapore's six-hour endurance, however, gave it an effective search radius of barely 200 miles. (IWM, CH 2556)

The area that could be searched effectively by British cruisers was often dramatically reduced by adverse weather. Here, the light cruiser HMS *Sheffield*, operating near the GIUK Gap in heavy seas, would have very little chance of spotting a German *Hilfskreuzer*. (IWM, A 14892)

too hard, lest they become dockyard cases. Thus, the limits of British cruiser endurance made it difficult for the Royal Navy to effectively cover the far reaches of the South Atlantic and Indian Ocean, which is precisely where the German *Hilfskreuzer* decided to hide.

The probability of British cruisers finding a German *Hilfskreuzer* solely with their own shipboard resources was depressingly poor. At 14 knots, a cruiser could move about 300 nautical miles per day and with decent weather and visibility, it could theoretically cover a search area of about 3,500 square miles. If it launched its Walrus seaplane at least once per day, it could increase its search area nearly ten-fold to about 35,000 square miles. Yet neither the older World War I cruisers nor the AMCs carried aircraft, and even the modern cruiser's search capabilities were drastically reduced at night or in poor weather. Thus, a *Kent*-class heavy cruiser on a 30-day patrol could theoretically search about one million square miles of ocean area. This seemingly impressive number, however, pales into insignificance when the vast areas of the South Atlantic, Indian Ocean, and Western Pacific, where the *Hilfskreuzer* operated, are considered – well over 50 million square miles. In the Indian Ocean, for example, the British typically had about 20 cruisers and AMCs available throughout 1941, but even if all were at sea, the Royal Navy could still search less than 2 percent of that ocean on a given day.

British cruisers built after 1920 carried anywhere from one to three Supermarine Walrus floatplanes for reconnaissance missions. These lightweight aircraft could either be launched directly from the cruiser's catapult or put over the side with the crane and take off directly from the water. Both launch and recovery required calm seas, and the cruiser to come to a dead stop for about 15 minutes, which limited the periods

Most British cruisers employed to hunt for raiders carried one or more Supermarine Walrus floatplanes, which could either be catapulted off the deck or lowered into the water for take-off. Although the Walrus only had a 4½ hour endurance, it gave cruiser captains a vital advantage in situational awareness when weather and sea conditions allowed them to be launched. The use of the Walrus proved critical in the destruction of the *Pinguin* and the *Atlantis*. (IWM, A 9271)

when the aircraft could be used. Once launched, the Walrus provided invaluable situational awareness to its cruiser by searching out to a radius of about 100 miles around its parent vessel, using a clockwise Vignot search pattern. Experienced British cruiser captains used their floatplanes to maximum advantage in searching for the *Hilfskreuzer*, but some regarded them as a nuisance that cluttered their decks.

Assuming that a *Hilfskreuzer* could be identified, the cruiser's firepower could give it a major advantage in a stand-up fight, if it fired first. The 8in/50 Mark VIII gun on the British heavy cruisers certainly gave them a big range advantage – a maximum of 30,000 yards versus no more than 16,400 yards for the German 15cm guns – as well as in weight of shot. Yet the low rate of fire of the 8in guns put them at a potential disadvantage in any fight under 11,000 yards, where the Germans could fire up to twice as many rounds per minute. Since German *Hilfskreuzer* carried 50 percent more ammunition than most British cruisers, they could afford to be profligate in a gunnery duel. The post-war British cruisers armed with the 6in/50 Mark XXIII also enjoyed a range superiority of at least 8,700 yards over the older German 15cm guns, and they could match them shot-for shot. The regular cruisers also had the advantage of the

TWIN 6IN MARK XXI TURRET ON HMAS *SYDNEY*

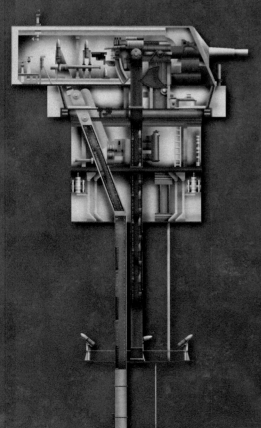

The twin 6in/50 guns on HMAS Sydney were breech loading, meaning that first a 112lb shell was loaded, followed by a 30lb cordite charge in a silk cloth bag.

Ammunition was brought up to the turret from the lower-deck magazine by means of two separate hoists, one for cordite charges and one for projectiles. Once in the turret, projectiles were moved by hand from the hoist and placed into the gun-loading tray, then rammed into the breech. Cordite charges varied, based on the range to target and were rammed in behind the projectile.

Each turret had a crew of 27 men.

Turrets are fired either in DIRECTOR or LOCAL control.

Entered Service: 1933
Rate of Fire: 5–6 rounds/minute
Maximum Range: 23,300m at 45°
Turret Train Rate: 5–7° per second
Muzzle Velocity: 841 m/sec
Ammo storage: 200 rounds per gun

British cruisers were usually armed with two quad torpedo tube launchers, located below the 4in AA gun deck. The Mark IX 21in torpedo had a range of 9,800–13,000 yards. HMAS *Sydney* fired a total of six torpedoes at much closer ranges against the *Kormoran*, but scored no hits. (IWM, A 7964)

more sophisticated DCT fire-control system, which enabled them to conduct effective standoff bombardment with considerable accuracy during daylight hours. In January 1941, selected cruisers began receiving the Type 284 surface fire-control radar that theoretically improved their ability to engage targets during periods of limited visibility, although this early system sometimes proved feckless in action.

At the other end of the cruiser spectrum, the older cruisers armed with 6in/45 Mark XII guns and the AMCs armed with obsolete 6in/45 Mark VII guns were inferior to the German 15cm guns in terms of both effective range and rate of fire. If a British cruiser could hit an unarmored *Hilfskreuzer*, even a few shells could blast their flimsy hulls apart, but the accuracy of British AMC gunners was not terribly good in 1941. Three different AMCs fired more than 1,000 rounds at *Thor* and scored only two non-critical hits, and even the *Kent*-class cruisers demonstrated a typical hit probability of only about 3 percent at medium ranges.

On the receiving end, most British cruisers built in the period 1920–1935 could not withstand much damage from 15cm guns or torpedoes if the *Hilfskreuzer* managed to catch them off guard. The poorly protected Treaty Cruisers were more vulnerable to a few lucky 15cm hits than some of the larger light cruisers. The Royal Navy had noticed the vulnerability of its bridge-mounted DCTs prior to the war and the inability of the back-up systems to control adequately the main armament, but due to limited budgets nothing was done to rectify the problem. Furthermore, the use of aluminum on valves and other critical fittings as a weight-saving measure left Treaty Cruisers vulnerable to fires within compartments, which could melt the aluminum components.

The interior of a 6in triple Mark XXIII mounting on board HMS *Jamaica* during a loading drill. All crew members are wearing anti-flash gear. The sailor in the foreground is lifting a 30lb cordite charge to the ammunition tray, while another cordite charge is just emerging from the hoist by his feet. (IWM, A 16320)

GERMAN

The *Hilfskreuzer* had five critical technical capabilities: its firepower, its mobility, its endurance, its ability to communicate with SKL in Berlin, and its ability to evade detection. Mission success and survival depended upon maintaining all five of these capabilities. When all were indeed functioning well, a *Hilfskreuzer* could be a very dangerous opponent, even for larger British cruisers.

Each *Hilfskreuzer* had a main battery of six 15cm SK L/45 cannon, but due to layout restrictions they could usually only fire a broadside of three guns at once. In combat, gunners on the *Hilfskreuzer* were trained to fire at maximum rate of fire to overwhelm an opponent in the opening moments, and these weapons could sustain a rate of 3–4 rounds per minute for up to about an hour. In extremis, the gun crews on *Thor* and *Kormoran* proved that they could fire up to 7 rounds per minute, although the weapons could not sustain this rate for very long without overheating. Recoil systems were also vulnerable to over-use and could put the gun out of battery, with the gun tube unable to recover from a recoil – a critical defect in combat.

Gun crews were able to sharpen their skills in frequent actions with merchant ships and most *Hilfskreuzer* were capable of pinpoint accuracy within 3,300–4,400 yards, enabling them to take out a ship's bridge and radio room with their opening salvo. In long-distance combat, a *Hilfskreuzer*'s 15cm batteries demonstrated a 5 percent hit probability at ranges around 8,700 yards and 1 percent probability at ranges of 15,000 yards and beyond. Each *Hilfskreuzer* carried 1,800 rounds of 15cm ammunition, most of which consisted of *Sprenggrenate* L/4.1 (high-explosive) rounds, although a few

A German 15cm gun crew drilling. The crews typically wore shorts and casual attire in the tropics. After months of practice against merchant ships, the gun crews on most raiders become very deadly at ranges of 10,000 yards and less. (Author's Collection)

armor-piercing rounds may have been carried. Against an unarmored merchant ship or AMC, the *Hilfskreuzer*'s main battery was effective out to 15,000 yards, but against an opponent with even modest armor, the 15cm battery only posed a serious threat within about 5,500 yards.

The main battery on a *Hilfskreuzer* was directed by a gunnery officer, who employed a 3m RU-Em optical rangefinder to determine distance. On the *Atlantis*, the rangefinder was hidden in a water tank above the wheelhouse. Since the large rangefinder could not be used before a raider dropped its disguise, the gunnery officer covertly employed a hand-held rangefinder during the approach to combat. Once the large rangefinder was unveiled, firing data was transmitted to the gun batteries by means of an elderly model 1910 telegraph system, allowing coordinated salvoes. Using stereoscopic rangefinders required a very well-trained gunnery staff, but allowed the *Hilfskreuzer* to get off rounds much quicker than the slower British system. Yet the fire-control system on *Hilfskreuzer* was very vulnerable to splinter damage and was not very effective beyond 12,000 yards.

Against enemy cruisers, the next most effective weapon was the ship's torpedo batteries, which had two 533mm tubes mounted on each side. Raiders carried the G7aT1 torpedo, which had a practical range of 6,500 yards at 44 knots but at slower settings could theoretically reach out to 15,000 yards. Typically, raiders launched torpedoes either in the opening moments of combat before their opponent could take evasive action or to finish off a crippled enemy ship. If the raider succeeded in hitting its opponent, the 660lb of Hexanite in the torpedo's warhead was sufficient to sink or cripple even a heavy cruiser. Most of the raiders, however, went to sea with torpedoes built very early in the war, before various defects were corrected, and consequently reliability was not always very good. Out of approximately 42 torpedoes launched by *Hilfskreuzer* in 1940–41, only 25 scored hits that inflicted damaged and most of these were against stationary targets. On July 29, 1941, the *Orion* launched a total of six torpedoes against the fleeing British freighter SS *Chaucer* at a range of less than 6,500 yards and scored only two hits, both of which failed to detonate. Against moving targets, German torpedo accuracy was especially poor, and *Kormoran* was the only one to score when it torpedoed HMAS *Sydney* at point-blank range.

A raider refueling at sea from a German supply ship. The Kriegsmarine's ability and willingness to conduct at-sea refueling was a critical enabler for *Hilfskreuzer* operations in the Indian Ocean and Pacific. Note the dog mascot on deck. (Author's Collection)

None of the *Hilfskreuzer* were particularly fast, with maximum speed ranging between 14 to 18 knots, which was often slower than some of the enemy merchant ships they were chasing. Yet the *Hilfskreuzer* had to have sufficient mobility to intercept the average merchantman and then to escape the area before British forces could arrive in response to their victim's radio calls. Several of the raiders, including *Widder*, *Orion*, and *Kormoran*, suffered persistent engine defects that caused them to shut down and drift for hours at sea while conducting repairs, increasing their vulnerability to British cruiser patrols. Yet except for the *Widder*, whose problematic engines eventually forced it to limp along at 7 knots, the rest of the *Hilfskreuzer* were able to maintain sufficient mobility to continue their missions.

The key constraint upon raider operations was the endurance of each ship, which varied considerably. *Widder* had the worst endurance, consuming 23 tons of fuel per day, which gave her an endurance of only 130 days. The more modern *Kormoran* was best suited for cruising, consuming only 8.5 tons per day, giving her a 352-day endurance. Unlike the Royal Navy, the Kriegsmarine incorporated at-sea logistics into its plans for commerce raiding, and each *Hilfskreuzer* could refuel at sea, as well as taking fuel oil from captured enemy tankers.

Ammunition was not a significant concern for most raiders, except for *Thor*, which expended 1,600 rounds of 15cm in its three battles with British AMCs. Water and food were a different matter. The *Atlantis* carried a four-month supply of fresh water for its 347-man crew, but stocks dwindled rapidly when hundreds of prisoners were captured. In practice, raiders needed water re-supply every three–four months or they faced strict water rationing, which could hurt shipboard morale. Maintaining morale was also at the heart of food resupply, since the *Hilfskreuzer* carried sufficient dry rations to last many months, but ship captains demanded that their crews receive fresh fruit, vegetables, and meat, as well as plenty of beer, every four months or so. Indeed, the German sailor's preference for fresh pork products resulted in numerous transfers of live pigs at sea between supply ships and raiders, in order to satisfy sailors isolated from the Fatherland for a year or more. The *Atlantis* war diary dutifully recorded eight such pig resupply deliveries between July 1940 and May 1941.

In order to conduct resupply, a raider had to communicate with the SKL in Berlin to arrange a rendezvous with a supply ship. The *Hilfskreuzer* also needed regular

Even when Allied aircraft spotted a *Hilfskreuzer*, they rarely could penetrate their disguise from normal search altitudes. Here, the *Atlantis*, disguised as a Dutch vessel, is seen from the air – and none of its armament is evident. (Author's Collection)

An Arado Ar 196-A floatplane being loaded aboard a raider. Although the wear and tear of launch and recovery caused a number of losses, the use of floatplanes provided the *Hilfskreuzer* with critical early warning about approaching Allied ships. (NARA)

intelligence and weather updates in order to avoid British warships and maximize their prospects for finding Allied shipping. Every day, the SKL transmitted instructions to each *Hilfskreuzer* during a specific three-hour period using the 100kW Norddeich transmitter near Bremen. Each raider had two Lorenz HF transmitters that it used to send *kurzsignal* (short signals) in special five-letter groups, encoded by its Enigma machine, to the SKL. Raiders also used captured British radios in order to broadcast fake distress calls.

Certainly the most essential characteristic of the *Hilfskreuzer* was the ability to avoid detection by superior British warships. The freighter *Goldenfels* was chosen because it bore a close resemblance to 26 other commercial vessels, and during its career as a *Hilfskreuzer*, *Atlantis* portrayed itself as ten different ships over the course of 20 months at sea. Each *Hilfskreuzer* carried large quantities of paint, canvas, timber, and foreign flags that enabled their crews to switch identities in just a few days. Typically, raider crews would add or subtract false funnels or bridge structures, and raise, lower, or omit masts to alter their appearance significantly. Even the 15cm guns were disguised as various deck structures. The crews were also trained to wear civilian clothes on deck, and usually there were special "characters" designed to make the vessel appear more harmless to a casual observer, such as a "woman" pushing a baby carriage on deck. German disguises fooled British patrols again and again. On May 18, 1941, the *Atlantis* – disguised as a Dutch freighter – passed within 8,000 yards of the British battleship HMS *Nelson* without arousing suspicion. British reconnaissance aircraft overflew *Hilfskreuzer* on several occasions, but they usually flew too high to detect subtle mistakes in the German camouflage.

Of course, the *Hilfskreuzer* wanted to avoid British warships whenever possible and only relied upon their disguises to aid them in the event of a surprise encounter. Captains preferred to gain additional security by aggressive use of their floatplanes, to find merchant targets and to warn them about enemy warships within 100 miles or so of the raider. The *Atlantis*, *Widder*, and *Pinguin* each carried Heinkel He 114B floatplanes, while the other four raiders carried the Arado Ar 196-A. The He 114B proved to be poorly suited for open ocean landings, and four of the six deployed were lost in accidents. Oftentimes, floatplanes were marked with British or French insignia so that they could pass as Allied aircraft, at least from a distance.

Raider name	Fuel consumption @ 10 knots (tons/day)	Days until refueling
Orion	20	145
Atlantis	12	250
Widder	23	130
Thor	13	166
Pinguin	18	207
Komet	11	193
Kormoran	8.5	352

STRATEGIC SITUATION

"Attack him where he is unprepared, appear where you are not expected."
– Sun Tzu

On September 6, 1939, three days after the Kriegsmarine authorized the use of *Hilfskreuzer* to disrupt British commerce, the Admiralty established the Northern Patrol to guard the Greenland–Iceland–UK (GIUK) Gap. Initially, the patrol consisted of the 7th and 12th Cruiser Squadrons with a total of eight elderly cruisers and they succeeded in intercepting a number of German merchant vessels trying to return to Germany. However, the C-, D-, and E-class light cruisers proved poorly suited to the rough seas in the North Atlantic and their endurance was too limited. Instead, the Admiralty began to substitute armed merchant cruisers for regular cruisers, and by February 1940 the Northern Patrol consisted solely of AMCs. Typically, a pair of AMCs such as HMS *Transylvania* and HMS *Scotstoun* patrolled the 180-mile wide Denmark Strait and several more in the Faroes Gap. Even though the AMCs were not equipped with search radar or floatplanes and the strait was often covered by fog, HMS *Transylvania* was able to intercept three homebound German freighters there between October 1939 and March 1940, so the Admiralty was confident that the GIUK Gap was secure. Based upon the Royal Navy's experience of intercepting three *Hilfskreuzer* in the North Sea during the World War I, the Admiralty believed that the Northern Patrol would limit the number of raiders that successfully broke out into the Atlantic.

The OKM intended to send out the first *Hilfskreuzer* in January 1940, but due to severe winter icing in the Baltic the first ships were not ready to sail until March. By the time that *Atlantis* and *Orion* sailed, the German invasion of Norway was underway and the Royal Navy was distracted away from the Denmark Strait. The next three raiders, *Widder*, *Thor*, and *Pinguin*, went through the Denmark Strait while the British were focused on the German invasion of France. Between April 6 and June 30, 1940, four raiders went through the Denmark Strait disguised as neutral Soviet freighters and one as a neutral Swedish freighter. Apparently, HMS *Transylvania* never spotted any of them. Thus, five of the raiders slipped through the British blockade at a time when the Royal Navy was thoroughly distracted and unaware that the AMCs were not a serious obstacle to the breakout of the German *Hilfskreuzer*. Although the Northern Patrol was reinforced by the time that the *Kormoran* slipped through the Denmark Strait on December 12/13, 1940, it still had significant gaps that German raiders were able to exploit.

The Kriegsmarine also decided to take advantage of the 1939 Molotov–Ribbentrop Pact, and hoped to send up to four raiders to the Pacific by means of passing through Soviet waters in the Arctic Sea. With the assistance of Soviet icebreakers, the *Hilfskreuzer Komet* began threading its way through the Arctic in August 1940 and eventually reached the Pacific by September. This route had the advantage of totally avoiding the British blockade, but Soviet cooperation was inconsistent and Stalin demanded a fee of 950,000 RM to assist with the *Komet*'s passage. As a result of the difficulties in getting the *Komet* through Soviet waters, the SKL decided not to deploy any more *Hilfskreuzer* via the northern route.

After the fall of France, Hitler wanted to force Britain to the negotiating table by attacking her trade shipping, using U-boats, long-range Fw 200 Condors and surface raiders. Yet most of these attacks were restricted to the North Atlantic and neither the U-boats nor the regular surface navy were able to mount more than occasional forays into the South Atlantic in 1940. The *Hilfskreuzer* provided the Kriegsmarine with a unique and cost-effective means to attack British trade in the South Atlantic, Indian Ocean, and Pacific, seas that would otherwise be inaccessible, and thereby deny Britain the luxury of "safe areas" beyond Germany's reach. The SKL assigned three specific missions to the *Hilfskreuzer*: sinking enemy vessels, disrupting British trade routes with its overseas empire, and forcing the Royal Navy to dispatch important naval resources to counter this threat.

Although the *Hilfskreuzer* operated far from home, the SKL made great efforts to create a Secret Naval Supply System (known as the *Etappendienst*) that enabled them to conduct a protracted campaign at sea. At the start of the war, 246 German merchant vessels were trapped overseas, including in friendly locations such as Japan and Brazil, which allowed some of these ostensibly "interned" vessels to move quietly in and out of their ports. A number of the more suitable freighters and tankers were activated as naval auxiliaries to supply the *Hilfskreuzer* in the remote Indian Ocean and Pacific. Japanese cooperation was low-key but significant. The SKL also asked the Italians in East Africa to assist the raider effort in the Indian Ocean, but their assistance was minimal.

In order for the *Etappendienst* to function, the raiders had to have covert locations where they could rendezvous with the supply ships in relative safety. Unlike U-boats, a *Hilfskreuzer* had to care for a significant number of prisoners each time it sank or captured enemy vessels, but this addition greatly increased the consumption of shipboard resources and could degrade a raider's freedom of action. Hence, the SKL developed plans to use remote islands and at-sea anchorages for covert supply rendezvous. One such point was known as "Andalusia" near the isle of Tristan de Cunha in the South Atlantic, which was first used by the *Graf Spee* to refuel from the *Altmark* in November 1939. The SKL was also very interested in Kerguelen in the Indian Ocean, which had been visited by the German survey ship SMS *Gazelle* in December 1874. The SKL obtained the *Gazelle's* detailed hydrographic charts of Kerguelen, and realized that the remote island could provide a valuable temporary base for the raiders. Unlike the Royal Navy, the Kriegsmarine understood that at-sea replenishment and refueling was a vital requirement in order to sustain protracted commerce raider operations in distant seas. Furthermore, the Admiralty's failure to appreciate these German logistical requirements severely hindered the Royal Navy's efforts to counter the commerce raider threat in 1940–41.

The bridge of the *Widder*. The tension – fueled by apprehension of a British cruiser appearing unexpectedly on the horizon – was often palpable among the deck crew and lookouts. (NARA)

Just as the *Hilfskreuzer* began to reach the open seas in the summer of 1940, the Royal Navy was stretched to its thinnest extent by the loss of Britain's French allies and the entry of Italy into the war. The bulk of the Royal Navy's cruisers were needed to protect the home islands from invasion, escort Atlantic convoys, and conduct fleet operations in the Mediterranean, which left precious little to watch the distant seas. Once merchant ships began disappearing in these areas in the summer of 1940, the Admiralty became aware that the blockade had failed to prevent the breakout of several raiders, and that it must now re-focus on trying to find and destroy them. The main responsibility for defeating the *Hilfskreuzer* fell upon the South Atlantic Command based in Freetown and the East Indies Command based in Ceylon. The China Station, based in Singapore and Hong Kong, as well as the Royal Australian Navy and Royal New Zealand Navy, would patrol their own waters and the Pacific. By the summer of 1940, the South Atlantic Command had six cruisers and eight AMCs, while the East Indies Command had three cruisers and four AMCs. The Pacific was guarded by eight cruisers and seven AMCs.

Initially, the Royal Navy believed that assigning cruisers to patrol the main shipping lanes would turn up chance contacts with raiders or at least put them in a position to respond to RRR reports from ships under attack. Unfortunately, only one-third of victims got off a warning, and even when they did most merchant vessels carried low-power radios with a typical range of only about 300 miles, meaning that QQQ and RRR signals were often not heard. Furthermore, the *Hilfskreuzer* became adept at sending out duplicate signals with the victim's call sign, but with a different location to confuse any

The crew of HMAS *Sydney* in 1941. The 645-man crew was well trained and had proven themselves in the Mediterranean. Not a single man survived the encounter with *Kormoran*. (Finding Sydney Foundation)

duplicate signals with the victim's call sign, but with a different location to confuse any nearby cruiser. Complicating matters, the Royal Navy had no fast and reliable means of confirming the identity of any civilian vessels encountered by patrolling cruisers. British captains relied upon the pre-war Talbot-Booth merchant ship recognition guide, which is the same reference that the SKL used to camouflage its raiders. Each cover identity that a *Hilfskreuzer* chose was of a ship that to which it bore a very close resemblance, at least in the guide. Although each merchant vessel had a unique radio call sign, this information was not carefully guarded in the first year of the war and it was relatively easy for raiders to assume the identities of real merchant vessels. It was not until December 1940 that the Admiralty decided to introduce a new system of secret call signs for each merchant ship in order to counter *Hilfskreuzer* false-flag tactics, but it took about a year

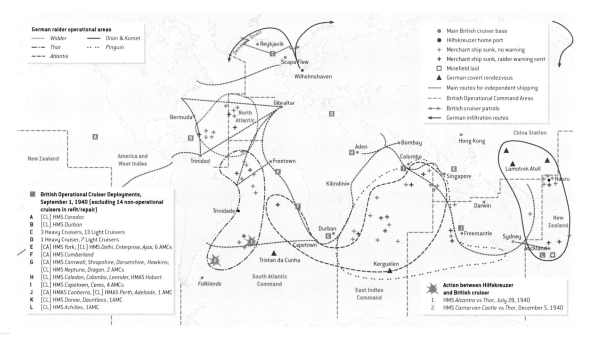

to implement the new procedures and they did not apply to neutral vessels.

Nor had the Admiralty staff seriously considered just what a raider looked like, an omission that soon proved to be quite a problem. It was not until January 1941 that the Admiralty gathered sufficient eye-witness reports from merchant marine sailors to publish CAFO 143, providing the first vague details to its cruiser captains on the likely armament of raiders. The difficulty in identifying raiders also seriously reduced the ability of the RAF or other Commonwealth air services to provide effective anti-raider reconnaissance. Coordination between the Royal Navy and the RAF was generally poor at the start of the war and no firm procedures were in place to spot raiders from the air. Nor did the RAF have many aircraft available for maritime patrol overseas, except for a few units such as 205 Squadron operating out of Singapore and Ceylon with out-dated flying boats. Australia and New Zealand each provided three maritime patrol squadrons, equipped with obsolete, short-ranged aircraft such as the Avro Anson or Blackburn Baffins. It was not until May 1940, when the Royal Australian Air Force (RAAF) and Royal New Zealand Air Force (RNZAF) maritime squadrons began to receive Lockheed Hudsons, that they could effectively patrol even their coastal areas. The RAF 205 Squadron received PBY Catalinas in mid 1941, but far too few to cover more than tiny portions of the Far East. The South Africa Air Force (SAAF) was in the worst shape materially, being forced to press 18 German-made Ju 86 aircraft into maritime patrol duty to cover the critical Cape of Good Hope. One Ju 86 had the satisfaction of sighting the German supply ship *Watussi* on December 2, 1939, and radioing its location to the nearby cruiser HMS *Sussex*, whose arrival forced the German to scuttle.

Without radar or effective air support, the British and Commonwealth cruisers assigned to overseas commerce protection had to rely primarily on shore-based naval

A crewman aboard the *Atlantis* demonstrates the rudimentary Soviet disguise adopted during the ship's breakout into the Atlantic in 1940. The Kriegsmarine cap band has been reversed to look Cyrillic and a red star has been added. Many of the Japanese disguises were similarly crude, but usually sufficient to deceive rudimentary inspections by passing British vessels and aircraft. (Author's Collection)

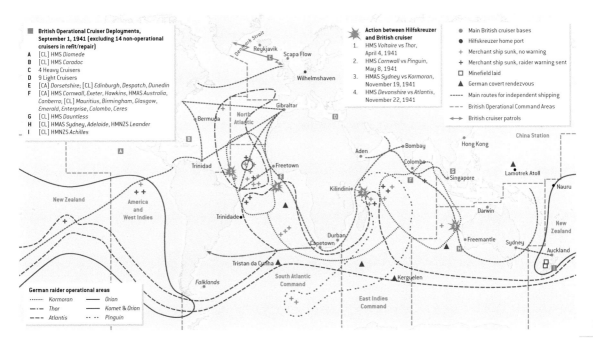

British Y-Service (signals intelligence) was capable of conducting direction finding (DF) and traffic analysis against German naval communications in 1940–41, providing broad clues about where German raiders were operating. Due to the robustness of the German naval Enigma codes, however, it was not until June 1941 and the capture of a number of Enigma machines and codebooks that the Y-Service actually began to read any of the messages. Furthermore, the code breakthroughs occurred against the *Heimisch* (Dolphin) code, which was used by U-boats and some supply ships in home waters, not by the raiders themselves. The *Hilfskreuzer* utilized the *Ausserheimisch* (Pike) Enigma cipher that was never broken by the British. The situation was further complicated in the Pacific, where the Royal Navy did not share Enigma-derived intelligence with the Australians or New Zealanders, who had no SIGINT capability of their own. Thus, British naval intelligence initially could only guess the general movements of the *Hilfskreuzer*.

Lacking proper strategic intelligence, the Royal Navy's overseas commands relied heavily upon operational intelligence provided by raider warnings, sightings of suspicious ships, and reports from ships' crews. Merchant ship captains were ordered to continue broadcasting the RRR signal as long as possible, which meant that the raider would undoubtedly shell the vessel to stop the communication. Here was a cold-blooded decision by the Admiralty to sacrifice merchant crewmen in the hope of gaining useful information about the location of raiders.

Back in Freetown, Ceylon, and Singapore, British naval staffs reacted to these signals by trying to dispatch the nearest cruiser or aircraft to the scene, although usually the raider was long gone by the time that these forces arrived. By 1941, the Admiralty ordered merchant captains to report any vessel that approached within a certain distance, which led to more false reports but also made it harder for the *Hilfskreuzer* to approach their victims. In 1940–41, however, only one-third of merchant ships attacked by raiders sent out a radio warning – most disappeared without a trace. Another key staff function was to develop a common operational picture about the merchant traffic operating in their region by means of a situation plot, since the *Hilfskreuzer* were usually pretending to be neutral ships that were actually elsewhere. Finally, the Royal Navy was able to gain considerable insight into raider operations by de-briefing Allied prisoners rescued from prize ships that were re-captured en route back to occupied Europe. While British operational intelligence got off to a shaky start in 1940, within a year it was beginning to refine its methods to provide the Royal Navy's cruisers critical information in a timely manner.

On the German side, the B-Dienst (a German naval codebreaking organization in Berlin) enjoyed some success in cracking British merchant codes, and the capture of so many merchant ships and prisoners by the *Hilfskreuzer* yielded significant information about British ship movements and signaling information. Pulling all this information together, B-Dienst and the SKL were able to gain great insight into British commercial and military movements in the Indian Ocean and South Atlantic, which helped the *Hilfskreuzer* to strike and evade detection for so long.

COMBATANTS

So now the Homeland wants us
to give of all we've got.
Our shells must let the Tommy know
'All seas' the German hand,
His throat to cut as gaily we
Behind the Führer stand.
The Indian Ocean's now our sphere
So, Tommy, do watch out!
– Gefreiter Kehrein, *Pinguin*, October 10, 1940

BRITISH/COMMONWEALTH

Both British heavy and light cruisers had an authorized complement of 650–720 men. The light cruiser HMAS *Sydney* had a 645-man crew in November 1941, of which 29 were officers. *Sydney*'s officers were an experienced group and only nine were reservists. However, the backbone of *Sydney*'s crew was her 58 petty officers, all but two of whom were pre-war, regular navy. Indeed, the average age of *Sydney*'s petty officers was 33, and more than 90 percent of them had at least six years' service in the navy. On British cruisers, there tended to more reservists and recent enlisted recruits, but there was an equally experienced cadre of pre-war officers and petty officers. Unlike the recently formed crews on the *Hilfskreuzer*, most cruiser sailors had served together aboard the same or similar vessels for many years.

CAPTAIN JOSEPH BURNETT, RAN (1899–1941)

Joseph Burnett was born in the town of Singleton near Sydney in December 1899. By the time that Burnett was 13, Australia was just beginning to establish its own navy and he was one of the first to enter midshipman training at the Royal Australian Naval College. After five years of training, the 17-year-old Midshipman Burnett was sent to England to join the crew of the battlecruiser HMAS *Australia*. Unfortunately, this vessel saw only limited service in the last two years of World War I, providing little practical experience for Burnett. After the end of the war, Burnett opted to remain attached to the Royal Navy for the next seven years, since it offered better chances for sea-going duty. In his spare time, he also honed his skills at tennis and was invited to play at Wimbledon.

Burnett steadily rose through the ranks, rising to lieutenant in 1920 and learning his trade as a gunnery officer. By 1924, Burnett was the gunnery officer aboard the light cruiser HMAS *Adelaide*, but he took time to return to Australia to get married. In 1927, he was promoted to lieutenant commander and assigned to the heavy cruiser HMAS *Canberra*, where he remained for the next four years. Reassigned to Naval Staff College in 1933, Burnett just missed the visit of Theodor Detmers aboard the *Canberra*.

After staff college, Burnett was promoted to commander in 1934 and spent nearly two years on shore duty in Melbourne. He did manage to return to *Canberra* as its executive officer in 1936 and a year later he went back to England to become executive officer of the

The British and Australian captains who fought the *Hilfskreuzer* were a fairly experienced group of regular navy officers, aged 41–49 in 1941. Yet most were new to independent command of a cruiser and their previous command experience – if any – often did not prepare them well for hunting down and destroying disguised raiders. For example, Captain Percival Manwaring of HMS *Cornwall* had previously commanded a minesweeper in home waters before being given command of a heavy cruiser in the Indian Ocean, but most

battleship HMS *Royal Oak*, but these were little more than short-term ticket-punching assignments. Afterwards, Burnett attended the Imperial Defence College and was promoted to captain just as war approached in Europe.

At the start of the war, Captain Burnett returned to Australia and became the Assistant Chief of Naval Staff at the Navy Office in Melbourne. For the next 20 months, Burnett was involved primarily in the mobilization of Australia's naval resources and was initimately involved in planning for the defense of Singapore and the Pacific region. Given his recent training at the Imperial Defence College, this assignment made perfect sense, but it did little to prepare him for command at sea. Burnett was a polished career officer and was evaluated as one of the "most promising and exceptional officers" in the Royal Australian Navy.

Burnett was finally able to secure another sea assignment, when he was given command of the light cruiser HMAS *Sydney* in May 1941. Although he had plenty of peacetime cruiser hours under his belt, Burnett had no previous command experience of any kind and no real wartime sea experience either, which made him rather a novice warship captain. Yet the crew of *Sydney* had seen plenty of action in the Mediterranean, and routine escort duties in Australian waters seemed like a safe way to allow a new captain to gain some experience before sending him into combat. During June–October 1941, *Sydney* escorted half a dozen convoys in Australian and New Zealand waters without any enemy contact. After six months of this routine duty, Burnett felt comfortable in his new command.

Unfortunately, Burnett appeared reticent to shake the crew out of the comfortable routine into which they settled while in home waters. When *Sydney* approached the vessel claiming to be the Dutch *Straat Malakka*, Burnett appears to have assumed that it was either a very ignorant Dutch vessel or at worst an enemy supply ship, neither of which he judged to be a threat to his 6in gun cruiser. Whatever else has been said about the ensuing action between *Sydney* and the *Kormoran*, it is clear that Detmers caught Burnett flat-footed. Like many British (and American) naval officers in the pre-war period, Burnett had followed a traditional career path better suited to preparing him for peacetime cruises rather than an unexpected fight to the death with a cunning opponent.

of his pre-war experience was staff duty ashore. Compared to the aggressiveness of the *Hilfskreuzer* captains, the British cruiser captains were generally more cautious and by-the-book, opting for methodical searches and waiting for a lucky break that might disclose the location of a raider. None of them knew very much about the methods or tactics of their opponents.

Cruiser crews had a significant advantage in morale over their German opponents. Their patrols usually lasted only a few weeks at sea before returning to a port for refueling, which meant that sailors had access to shore leave and regular rations. For Australian and New Zealand cruiser sailors, they were often operating from their home ports. Unlike the Germans, the British and Australian crews also benefited from the fact that they were operating in friendly waters, with reinforcements and support fairly close at hand. In mid 1941, cruiser crews in the Indian Ocean and Pacific did not have to worry much about enemy attack, which reduced the stress level considerably compared to the crews of *Hilfskreuzer*, who were always apprehensive that an enemy cruiser would suddenly appear on the horizon. Nor did the cruiser crews need to take care of hundreds of prisoners aboard ship or worry about running out of water.

OPPOSITE
The officers of the heavy cruiser HMS *Kent* playing deck hockey out in the open air next to the 8in gun turrets while in Scapa Flow in October 1941. By late 1941, one-third of British cruisers were laid up in port due to battle damage and mechanical repairs, which gave many crews a breather from constant patrolling. (IWM, A 7605)

The loneliness of command at sea. Here, the captain of the cruiser HMS *Suffolk* during the pursuit of the *Bismarck* in May 1941. Pursuit of *Hilfskreuzer* and their supply ships often required weeks of monotonous patrolling and it was easy for crews to fall into a routine that could one day be fatal.
(IWM, A 4330)

Of all the cruisers that hunted the *Hilfskreuzer*, HMAS *Sydney* had the most experienced crew, the vessel having compiled an impressive war record in the Mediterranean during June 1940–January 1941. In six months, *Sydney* played a major role in sinking an Italian light cruiser and a destroyer, as well as destroying a four-ship convoy and participating in numerous shore bombardments. Her gunnery officer, Lieutenant-Commander Michael M. Singer, was an experienced officer on loan from the Royal Navy. In comparison, many of the cruisers assigned to anti-raider duties in 1940–41, such as HMS *Cornwall*, HMS *Devonshire*, and HMS *Dorsetshire*, spent much of the first year of the war on relatively quiet convoy escort duty in backwaters. Shipboard training was based on recurrent practical drills for gunnery and damage control, but did not anticipate point-blank battles with disguised raiders.

In contrast, the crews on AMCs, each usually about 200–300 in number, were assembled in September–November 1939 from a mix of regular Royal Navy, reservists, and merchant sailors. Each AMC had about 20 officers, mostly from the Royal Naval Reserve (RNR) or Royal Naval Volunteer Reserve (RNVR), and about a dozen petty officers, mostly from the regular navy. Often the merchant sailors serving aboard pre-war passenger ships were simply reclassified as Naval Auxiliary Personnel (MN). After a brief period of training ashore, the crews were quickly dispatched to their patrol areas. Patrolling waters like the Denmark Strait for three weeks at a stretch was a dreary as well as hazardous duty, since remaining in the same area for so long made the AMCs highly vulnerable to U-boats. One AMC sailor commented that at least "icebergs were common, and handy for target practice." Even though the Admiralty tried to limit the AMCs to defensive missions, by the end of 1940 two had been sunk by German warships and eight by U-boats, with the loss of more than 600 crewmen. In comparison, only two regular light cruisers had been sunk by enemy action. British sailors assigned to AMCs soon dubbed them "Admiralty-Made-Coffins," and felt that the Royal Navy regarded both the ships and the crews as expendable.

The captains of the AMCs were almost entirely drawn from retired Royal Navy officers, many with distinguished records in World War I. Unfortunately, a bit of wartime experience under their belts tended to make the AMC captains more aggressive than they should have been with vessels that were only quasi-warships. This aggressiveness was demonstrated again and again, when AMC captains chose to engage stronger enemy warships rather than to play for time and await reinforcements.

GERMAN

Schiff 16, also known as the *Atlantis*, had a crew of 20 officers, 70 non-commissioned officers (NCOs), and 278 enlisted men, for a total of 368. Kapitän zur See Bernhard Rogge, his executive officer, and the gunnery officer were all regular navy, but many of the other positions were filled by reservists and experienced personnel drawn from the merchant marine. Given that the *Hilfskreuzer* were masquerading as merchant vessels, it made sense to include a number of experienced mariners in the crew to ensure that the vessel looked and acted like a civilian ship. Initially, the Kriegsmarine personnel depots tried to fob off sub-standard recruits on the *Hilfskreuzer*, which were regarded by some as expendable ships, but Rogge and the other raider captains successfully pressured the SKL to supply high-quality personnel. Indeed, Rogge rejected nearly half the initial batch of recruits sent to join the *Atlantis*. Three of the raider captains – Rogge, Otto Kähler on *Thor*, and Kurt Weyher on the *Orion* – had commanded one of the Kriegsmarine's sail training ships just before the war, and they used their knowledge of recent training cruises to select some of the very best people available. Each captain sought capable volunteers with a broad range of skills, and since the crews were formed early in the war, the personnel came from the cream of the pre-war navy, reservists, and merchant marine.

The crew of each *Hilfskreuzer* was divided into two divisions for watch purposes. Ship's armament was controlled by a gunnery

FREGATTENKAPITÄN THEODOR DETMERS (1902–76)

Theodor Detmers was born in the town of Witten in the Ruhr in August 1902. Despite the fact that his father was a merchant and that prospects for military service after Germany's defeat in World War I seemed poor, at age 19 Detmers decided to join the Reichsmarine in April 1921. Detmers served his initial period of training as a Fähnrich (midshipman) on two different pre-dreadnoughts and then a training ship in the Baltic.

In October 1925, Detmers was promoted to Oberfähnrich (sub-lieutenant) and posted to the brand-new light cruiser *Emden*. He participated in the *Emden*'s first international cruise, sailing around Africa to the Indian Ocean. Afterwards, he was assigned to shore duty for two years, but then sent to the torpedo boat *Albatross* as a Leutnant in 1928. In 1932, he was promoted to Kapitänleutnant and transferred to the light cruiser *Koln*, on which he went on another international cruise through the Mediterranean and Suez Canal to the Indian Ocean, Australia, China, and Japan. On May 9, 1933, the *Koln* docked in Sydney and he and other German officers were invited aboard the cruiser HMAS *Canberra* for a reception. Upon returning to Germany, Detmers was given command of a torpedo boat in 1934 and then the new destroyer *Z7 Hermann Schoemann* in October 1938.

A year later Germany was at war, and Korvettenkapitän (commander) Detmers participated in multiple anti-

commerce and mine-laying operations in the North Sea during the first six months of the war. Recurring engine

and torpedo officer and the weaponry was operated by about 75 crewmen. On *Atlantis*, two officers and 64 men were assigned to the engine spaces, with a navigation officer and eight steersman available for bridge duty. Three watch officers and nine signalmen were also assigned to the bridge and served as the primary lookouts. Unlike British cruisers, which often used only a single lookout aloft, the *Hilfskreuzer* put three lookouts up in a disguised crows nest on the main mast; no raider captain wanted to trust his ship's survival to a single man's eyesight. *Atlantis* had an unusually large radio section, with 27 personnel, including a signals intelligence detachment from B-Dienst, which would improve the raider's situational awareness about British communications in its vicinity. Given that *Hilfskreuzer* could not expect much support at sea, they also carried large numbers of technicans (five carpenters and 23 mechanics on *Atlantis*) and a robust medical staff (two doctors and five medics). The ship's flight detachment numbered a pilot and four support personnel.

problems and a collision with another destroyer limited his ship's contributions, and his destroyer was laid up during the initial invasion of Norway in April 1940. In June 1940, however, Detmers' destroyer participated in Operation *Juno*, a fleet sortie off the coast of Norway. When some British shipping was intercepted, Detmers was ordered to finish off the damaged 5,666-ton British tanker *Oil Pioneer* with a torpedo – his first "kill."

Returning from Operation *Juno*, Detmers was surprised to discover that the SKL had re-assigned him to the *Hilfskreuzer* HSK-8 Schiff 41, soon to be re-named *Kormoran*. Detmers had long been interested in *Hilfskreuzer* operations, but he thought that at 38 he was too young for such an independent command. Aside from Kurt Weyher on the *Orion*, all the other captains were 40–51 years of age with greater sea experience. Yet the SKL had chosen well, and Detmers proved to be a tough, disciplined commander who was well suited for independent raiding operations.

After the ship went through two months of work-up in the Baltic, Detmers took *Kormoran* to sea in December 1940. Detmers preferred to eat in the mess with his men – a habit he had acquired in the close quarters aboard torpedo boats and destroyers. He was a bit of an ascetic and a teetotaller, forbidding the use of hard liquor and encouraging regular exercise for the crew. Detmers excelled at raiding operations, taking 11 ships of 68,000 tons in the South Atlantic and Indian Ocean. He also twice managed to evade British AMCs that spotted his raider and came after him in hot pursuit. Detmers' pre-war knowledge of these waters and British cruiser operations was invaluable in enabling his vessel to survive for so long. When finally cornered by HMAS *Sydney*, Detmers demonstrated superior cunning and tactical ability that allowed him to dominate the action against his better-armed opponent.

After the loss of the *Kormoran* in November 1941, Detmers and most of his crew were held in a POW camp north of Melbourne for the next six years. During his imprisonment, Detmers learned that Hitler had awarded him the *Ritterkreuz des Eisernen Kreuzes* (Knight's Cross of the Iron Cross) for his feat of sinking the *Sydney*. Detmers was able to resist the relentless interrogation and conceal some details of the final battle with HMAS *Sydney*. Once Japan was in the war, Detmers tried to escape in the hope of reaching Japanese-held Indonesia, but the attempt failed. Captivity was hard on Detmers and in 1944 he suffered a stroke that left him incapacitated. He was finally released in 1947 but due to poor health, he could not serve in the post-war *Bundesmarine* as Rogge did. Detmers spent the next three decades living quietly in Hamburg and wrote his memoirs in 1959.

Many of the regular officers and sailors assigned to the *Hilfskreuzer* came from minesweepers, torpedo boats, naval auxiliaries, or training ships in the Baltic, which meant that they were accustomed to short-duration patrols. The former merchantmen in the crews added significant overseas experience, including knowledge of foreign ports and commercial routes. Most crews received some training at Bremerhaven while their vessels were fitting out and then some limited gunnery training in the Baltic, but given the need for secrecy there were no real "shake-out" cruises prior to operational deplyment. Few crewmen had any combat experience before their cruises and the initial encounter between the *Atlantis* and the freighter SS *Scientist* was marred by poor gunnery and sloppy execution. Yet after a year at sea together, the *Hilfskreuzer* crews became experts at seamanship,

Bernhard Rogge as a Vizeadmiral next to his flagship *Prinz Eugen* in March 1945. He is wearing the *Ritterkreuz des Eisernen Kreuzes mit Eichenlaub* (Knight's Cross of the Iron Cross with Oakleaves) awarded for the successful cruise of the *Atlantis*. Rogge was actually one-quarter Jewish and nearly driven from the Kriegsmarine before being issued a *Deutschblütigkeitserklärung* (German blood certificate) from Hitler just before he took command of the *Atlantis* in 1939. Rogge's wife, however, committed suicide due to harassment by the Nazis and this must have had some affect on his attitude toward the regime he served. (Author's Collection)

gunnery, and evading detection. On *Atlantis*, the crew mastered the art of re-painting the ship's hull at sea – no mean feat – and reconfiguring the ship's appearance in just a couple of days. The crews also had to get accustomed to operating in a wide range of environmental conditions, ranging from frigid Arctic waters to tropical heat in the Indian Ocean. Constant attacks on merchant shipping gradually honed the raider crews to a razor edge, which made them into very dangerous opponents.

Leadership on the *Hilfskreuzer* was aggressive and independent. Unlike normal fleet units, raider captains had wide discretion and usually only received broad guidance about operational areas from the SKL by radio. Surrounded by enemies and operating far from home, circumstances forced the raider captains to survive based on their cunning and ingenuity, not by slavishly following orders.

Certainly the greatest challenge facing the crews of the *Hilfskreuzer* was the unprecedented length of their patrols, which were expected to last at least a year. In comparison, U-boat patrols to the South Atlantic in 1941 lasted only 60–90 days. Morale aboard ship was initially very high, given the high caliber of the crews, but even vessels like *Atlantis* began to suffer some deterioration of morale after 12 months at sea. Since the *Hilfskreuzer* tended to operate in the deep blue away from Allied-held shorelines, it was not uncommon that crews spent months without sight of land, which increased their sense of isolation. At best, the *Hilfskreuzer* sailor might get a few days ashore in some barren island like Kerguelen. Lack of contact with women for over a year and irregular mail from home (delivered by the occasional supply ship) were the biggest poison for morale, and on *Atlantis* Rogge had to deal with several instances of homosexual misconduct and misbehavior caused by homesickness. Close contact with large numbers of enemy prisoners, who consumed their finite food and water supplies at a prodigious rate, was also upsetting for the crew. Sensitive to this gradual slump in morale, *Hilskreuzer* captains made great efforts to ensure that their crews received plenty of "comfort" rations such as beer from Japan, fresh fruit, vegetables, and pork. Indeed, when the amount of food captured from Allied merchant vessels is taken into account, it is doubtful that any other German combatants in World War II ate as well as the raider crews. *Kormoran's* crew enjoyed a swimming pool in one of the cargo holds and many ships encouraged boxing competitions, even between Kriegsmarine sailors and enemy prisoners. When in tropical waters, Otto Kähler allowed his sailors on *Thor* to go on watch in swimming trunks. When incentives failed to improve morale, malcontents were sent home on prize vessels or supply ships. It was only when a ship and crew were reaching the breaking point that the SKL would order them to return home.

COMBAT

"They've blown the wireless room to hell"
– Lieutenant Llewellyn, HMS *Voltaire*, April 4, 1941

THOR VS. HMS *ALCANTARA*, JULY 28, 1940

On the morning of June 16, 1940, Otto Kähler's *Thor* reached the North Atlantic and began proceeding south toward his operational area in the South Atlantic. He soon reached the busy shipping lanes off the Brazilian coast and between 1 and 17 July the *Thor* captured or sank seven merchantmen totaling more than 35,000 tons. Amazingly, only one of Kähler's seven victims was able to send out a QQQ raider warning before German gunfire silenced their radio. Even more surprising, the one warning sent was not heard by any British stations, and the Admiralty was not aware for days that these ships were sunk, which allowed *Thor* to get clean away from each kill. The raider *Widder*, which was also operating off the northeast coast of Brazil, eliminated four merchantmen in this area.

It was not until July 17 that Rear Admiral Henry Harwood, in command of the South America Division assigned to protect trade off Brazil, was made aware that there was some German naval activity heading his way. The Y-Service had DF'ed a German naval transmitter near the Cape Verde Islands, although it could not determine if it was a U-boat or a raider. British Naval Intelligence also noted that the German tanker *Rekum* had slipped out of the Spanish port of Tenerife and might be heading for a link-up with a raider. What Harwood did not know was that both *Widder* and *Thor* were active off Brazil, as well as U-boats. The only units available to

A German wartime postcard depicts the *Thor* in action against a British AMC. *Thor* lacked the speed to outrun the faster AMCs and depended upon superior gunnery and a bit of luck to decide the issue. (Author's Collection)

Harwood to search for the possible raider were the elderly cruiser HMS *Hawkins* and the AMC HMS *Alcantara*. Perhaps basing his decision on his previous run-in with the *Graf Spee* seven months earlier, Harwood decided to keep the *Hawkins* close to the Brazilian coast to protect the shipping lanes around Rio, while sending Captain John Ingham's *Alcantara* out more than 250 miles from the coast to inspect the uninhabited Trinidade Island. British intelligence believed that this remote island might be used by a German raider, but *Alcantara* reached the island on July 26 and found nothing.

Two days later, the *Alcantara* was steaming eastward at 11 knots when her lookouts spotted a vessel on the horizon around 1000hrs. It was *Thor*, disguised as the Yugoslav freighter *Vir*. At first, Kähler turned toward the approaching vessel, thinking it was a large cargo ship, but as the range closed it became clear that it was an AMC. Instead of trying to bluff his way past the British cruiser, Kähler swung *Thor* about and increased speed to 15 knots. This act only confirmed that the fleeing ship was probably hostile, which caused Ingham to increase speed and broadcast a radio alert about the suspicious vessel. *Thor* tried to jam the signal, which further confirmed her hostile nature. Kähler had made a serious mistake, because the *Alcantara* had a 4–5-knot speed advantage over her, and it was obvious that *Alcantara* was calling for reinforcements. The stern chase went on for three hours, with *Alcantara* gradually closing the distance. With many hours of daylight left and the enemy gaining on him, Kähler had no choice but to turn and fight before reinforcements arrived.

At 1300hrs, *Alcantara* was within 17,500 yards and began to send a blinker signal asking, "What ship?" Kähler responded by ordering a turn hard to starboard and unveiling his armament and Kriegsmarine colors. One minute later, a two-gun ranging salvo was fired, followed by three four-gun salvoes in rapid succession. Despite firing at the maximum range of their 15cm guns, the German gunners scored five hits in the opening eight minutes of the action. One hit knocked out *Alcantara*'s primary fire control director (FDC) and the wireless, another disabled a 6in gun, and another hit the waterline, causing flooding in the starboard engine room. *Alcantara* replied with several 6in gun salvoes, but the effective range of Ingham's old 6in guns was only 15,000 yards and loss of director control made their fire slow and inaccurate. Ingham had made the mistake of getting too close, when he could have achieved his mission merely by staying in contact with *Thor* until a regular cruiser arrived. Instead, the flooding in the engine room caused *Alcantara* to slow down to 10 knots, meaning that she could no longer keep up with *Thor*. Seeing his enemy slowing after several hits and their fire slackening, Kähler made his second mistake by deciding to close the distance – perhaps he could finish this opponent off, after all. *Alcantara*'s gunners, however, shifted to their secondary fire control and with the range closing they managed to score a 6in hit on *Thor* that punched through its upper hull near the stern without exploding.

Kähler had had enough. He dropped smoke floats and beat a hasty retreat to the south, but *Alcantara* managed to score one more hit on *Thor*'s boat deck that knocked out the torpedo battery's fire control and killed three sailors and wounded four more. With two dead, seven wounded and significant damage, Ingham turned his ship about and headed for Rio. During the 35-minute action, *Thor* fired 284 15cm rounds and achieved eight hits, while *Alcantara* had fired 152 rounds and scored two hits. This action was one that the British should have won, because Kähler had foolishly thrown away the advantages of disguise and could not escape from a faster opponent in daylight. Once Harwood received the *Alcantara*'s sighting report, the cruiser HMS *Dorsetshire* was dispatched from Freetown to intercept. If *Alcantara* had shadowed *Thor* and vectored in the *Dorsetshire*, the German raider's fate would have been sealed.

The AMC HMS *Alcantara*, which fought the *Hilfskreuzer Thor* on July 28, 1940. Despite getting the worse of the action, the AMC hit *Thor* twice and inflicted seven casualties – the only combat casualties that the Royal Navy managed to inflict on a *Hilfskreuzer* in 1940. (IWM, FL 386)

THOR VS. HMS *CARNARVON* CASTLE, DECEMBER 5, 1940

After evading *Alcantara*, *Thor* repaired her damage, buried her dead, and changed her identity. As British intelligence suspected, *Thor* did rendezvous with the tanker *Rekum*, as did *Widder*. Kähler laid low for a few weeks to avoid the expected British dragnet, but there was little sign of enemy activity. In late September, the *Thor* resumed operations off the Brazilian coast and eliminated two more large merchant vessels in two weeks, before encountering a "dry spell" in which no targets were encountered. The crew settled into a dull routine for the next eight weeks, waiting for supply ships and more valuable targets.

Meanwhile, the South Atlantic Command was busy rallying its forces to search for the elusive raiders, and by November there were ten cruisers out searching for the *Thor*. The AMC HMS *Carnarvon Castle*, under Captain Henry Hardy, was assigned to patrol about 200 miles out from Montevideo; at 0642hrs on the morning of December 5, it spotted a suspicious vessel heading away at a range of 19,000 yards. Hardy ordered an intercept course and had his signalman send the query "What ship?" Once again, Kähler decided to drop all pretenses and run for it. The identity check was ignored. Within moments, Hardy was aware that he had encountered an enemy vessel and broadcast a sighting report. Kähler was in exactly the same situation as he had been with the *Alcantara* – a stern chase with a faster opponent who was calling for reinforcements. He was also close enough to Montevideo to realize that another British cruiser might soon arrive, before nightfall gave him a chance to shake his pursuer.

Hardy proved to be just as over-aggressive as Ingham, gradually closing the range over the next hour to 17,000 yards and opting to engage his fleeing opponent rather than just shadowing. *Carnarvon Castle* was faster than *Thor*, but the German 15cm guns had a significant advantage over the British 6in guns in terms of range and rate of fire. Hardy ordered a one-round ranging shot at 0757hrs, followed by a four-gun salvo one minute later. Firing at a target presenting its stern beyond maximum range had little chance of scoring any hits, but it did convince Kähler to turn and fight. This time, he opted for a circular course to starboard in order to bring the maximum armament to bear on the approaching cruiser. Laying smoke to hinder *Carnarvon Castle*'s aim, *Thor* began a gradual turn to starboard, but kept firing back with its three stern guns. The *Carnarvon Castle* continued to bang away with its forward 6in guns, but scored no hits.

As his opponent closed in, Kähler suddenly turned hard to starboard at 0838hrs and fired two torpedoes at *Carnarvon Castle*. Despite a sharp deflection angle, the torpedoes passed within 50 yards of the AMC on either side – an unnerving experience to be sure. *Thor*'s four-gun broadsides now began to score repeatedly on *Carnarvon Castle*, smashing its wireless and knocking out its fire control. By 0900hrs, with his ship a burning wreck and four of his crew killed and 32 wounded, Hardy decided to turn away from his opponent and break off the action. Kähler obliged

HMS *Carnarvon Castle*, which engaged *Thor* on December 5, 1940. The liner's high sides made an excellent target and *Thor*'s gunners scored 27 hits before the AMC broke off the action. (Author's Collection)

him, but continued to pour on 15cm fire and scored more hits at ranges between 9,000–11,000 yards. With a significant list, *Carnarvon Castle* laid smoke and fled the scene. During the 75-minute action, the *Thor* fired 593 rounds and achieved 27 hits, but *Carnarvon Castle* failed to score a single hit after firing over 600 rounds. It seemed that neither side had learned from the previous duel, since Kähler opted for another hopeless stern chase while the British AMC captain chose to forego his mission of shadowing the raider until reinforcements arrived. Instead, superior German gunnery decided the issue and delivered a clear tactical victory.

With her radio disabled, the *Carnarvon Castle* was not immediately able to inform the Admiralty of the results of this action, which allowed *Thor* to get clean away again. Nevertheless, within two days the South Atlantic Command was aware of the battle and it happened to have a ready response force at hand. On October 31, the pocket battleship *Admiral Scheer* had run the Denmark Strait and proceeded toward the South Atlantic; in response, the South Atlantic Command formed a hunting group composed of the cruisers HMS *Cumberland*, *Enterprise*, and *Newcastle* to patrol the waters off Brazil. All three cruisers were sent forthwith toward the area of the battle between *Carnarvon Castle* and *Thor*, but after a week of fruitless searching they were redirected back to the search for the *Scheer*. If Captain Hardy had shadowed the *Thor* properly on December 5, the hunting group would almost certainly have been able to corner this raider.

Meanwhile, the *Thor* evaded her pursuers and headed eastward toward the Cape of Good Hope. *Thor*'s ammunition and fuel were severely depleted after the battle with *Carnarvon Castle* and she was urgently in need of resupply. The SKL directed the *Thor* toward the tanker *Eurofeld* to refuel, and then to Point Andalusia between Brazil and Africa, where on December 26 *Thor* met the *Admiral Scheer* and the raider *Pinguin*. Psychologically it was comforting to be around other German ships, but it was tactically unsound for a disguised raider to remain in close company with other vessels, so each vessel was assigned its own operating area in the South Atlantic. Kähler spent most of the winter months prowling, but failed to find any new targets. During this time, *Thor* met with resupply vessels seven times and received additional fuel, ammunition, and foodstuffs, but the lack of contact with enemy shipping was frustrating.

THOR VS. HMS *VOLTAIRE*, APRIL 9, 1941

After three months without any action, *Thor* finally encountered and sank two enemy vessels on March 25, 1941. One of these was the passenger liner SS *Britannia*, which Kähler sank with gunfire after it sent out an RRR raider report. Signalmen on the *Thor* heard a British vessel, apparently only a few hours distant, respond to the signal and reply that it was en route. Kähler feared it was a British cruiser racing toward him so he decided to depart post haste, leaving the 527 passengers in their lifeboats and assumed they would be picked up by the approaching vessel. Instead, the survivors spent up to three weeks in the water and almost 200 perished. Later, Kähler found out about this loss of life from a British radio broadcast and it caused him to reconsider his methods.

On April 4, *Thor* was disguised as a Greek freighter and was back in familiar waters northeast of Brazil, when her lookouts spotted smoke off to port on the horizon at 0615hrs. The smoke was from HMS *Voltaire* under Captain James A. Blackburn, assigned independent patrol duty west of the Cape Verde islands. Kähler decided to turn toward the unknown vessel for a closer inspection. Blackburn spotted *Thor*, but assumed it was a small freighter and also turned to identify it, placing *Voltaire* nearly bows-on to *Thor* at a distance of about 15,000 yards. Neither ship could immediately identify the other. Kähler figured he was dealing with another passenger ship and when the distance closed to 9,000 yards at 0645hrs, he ordered his forward 15cm gun to fire a warning shot across the stranger's bow. Unexpectedly, the unknown vessel returned fire from two guns. There must have been imprecations uttered on the bridge of *Thor* when Kähler suddenly realized that he had mistakenly challenged another AMC. This time, the ships were on a converging course well within gunnery range, and Kähler knew that he had no choice but to fight it out.

Thor's experienced gunners quickly decided the action. The first four-gun salvo smashed the *Voltaire*'s radio room before it even had a chance to send out an RRR report, as well as the primary fire control. Within four minutes the ship was ablaze. Signalman Roger V. Coward, in his book *Sailors in Cages* (1967), described the scene on *Voltaire*:

The *Voltaire* was bumping and thudding in a horribly eccentric way, with engines full speed ahead, and her decks were like a China shop after the bull had left – an absolute shambles. Men who had been caught in the blast and by the fearful hail of shrapnel

which scythed men like grass, were thrown about in blood and confusion. Some were no more than rags of dead flesh… I staggered again to the upper deck, where dead and injured were everywhere now. The ship was being riddled with holes, on fire amidships, in a pall of heavy smoke.

With the primary rangefinder destroyed, *Voltaire's* 6in gun fire rapidly became slow and uncoordinated, allowing *Thor* to gain firepower superiority over its opponent. Coward recalled:

A raider firing a 21in torpedo from a twin launcher. Most of the raider captains had strong backgrounds in mine and torpedo warfare and this was their weapon of choice against a British cruiser. The G7aT1 torpedo of 1940–41, however, was rarely effective beyond a range of a few thousand yards. (NARA)

> The guns were red-hot. Hoses were being played on them to keep them in action … a shell fragment hit one of the stern guns just as the crew was putting a load of cordite into the breech. There was a hellish flash and explosion, and all the crew were instantly reduced to a mass of ashes. Amidst all this carnage, I was struck by the incongruity of the stewards taking soup and sandwiches to the gun crews.

At 0715hrs, *Voltaire's* steering gear was hit and the burning ship began to helplessly circle at 13 knots. With his bridge ablaze, Captain Blackburn went to the stern personally to direct one of the two remaining 6in gun mounts still in action, but only succeeded in blasting off the top of the raider's mast. Kähler decided to fire two torpedoes from the extreme range of 7,000 yards, both of which missed. Yet it was apparent that the *Voltaire* was mortally wounded, and around 0800hrs Blackburn gave orders to abandon ship. At 0835hrs, the burning *Voltaire* rolled over and sank. Kähler rescued Captain Blackburn and 188 of his men, but 76 British sailors had been killed or died of wounds. During the 55-minute action, *Thor* fired an incredible 724 rounds and scored dozens of hits, without suffering any significant damage itself.

After the experience with the *Britannia*, Kähler decided to stay in the area for five hours to search for survivors, despite the likelihood that other British warships were nearby. He then headed north, changed his ship's disguise again, refueled from the tanker *Ill*, and began the journey back to Europe. German radio proudly announced the sinking of *Voltaire*, but omitted the identity of the victor. On April 30, the *Thor* safely reached Hamburg. In the course of *Thor's* 329-day cruise, Kähler had fought three AMCs and either prevailed or avoided defeat in all three actions.

THE DUEL IN THE INDIAN OCEAN, JUNE 1940–APRIL 1941

Outbound nine weeks from Gotenhafen, the raider *Pinguin* entered the Indian Ocean on August 20, 1940, disguised as the Greek freighter *Kassos*. Fregattenkapitän Ernst-Felix Krüder's *Pinguin* was only the second *Hilfskreuzer* to reach the Indian Ocean,

after Bernhard Rogge's *Atlantis* began operations there in June. South African air patrols from bases around the Cape of Good Hope failed to detect the new raider and the first inkling the East Indies Command had of Krüder's presence was when he began attacking shipping south of Madagascar. In quick succession, *Pinguin* sank two tankers and a freighter, but one merchant captain managed to send a QQQ signal. In response, Vice-Admiral Sir Ralph Leatham, commander of the East Indies Command in Colombo, dispatched the cruisers *Neptune* from Durban and *Colombo* from Aden, as well as two AMCs, to search for the raider. Unfortunately, only *Neptune* had a floatplane and the British search found nothing but an oil slick from one of *Pinguin*'s victims. During this period, Leatham assigned most of his cruisers to escort troopship convoys to Suez, rather than go flailing around the Indian Ocean in search of occasional RRR signals. Even worse, Leatham's intelligence staff had no idea where the raiders would strike next.

From June to November 1940, the *Atlantis* and the *Pinguin* picked off 22 Allied merchant ships totaling 161,200 tons. Both raiders were coordinated by radio from the SKL and were kept well informed about British naval dispositions. Leatham's meager search efforts, with only a handful of cruisers and aircraft, did not seriously press the two *Hilfskreuzer*. Rogge and Krüder knew that as long as they kept their distance from British bases, the chances of being intercepted were slim.

The two raiders conducted an at-sea rendezvous for two days north of Kerguelen Island on December 8, 1940, to coordinate their operations better. Six days later, *Atlantis* became the first raider to utilize the abandoned French whaling base at Kerguelen and Rogge remained there nearly a month over Christmas. Kerguelen proved to be important as a place for the raiders to acquire fresh water from the glaciers, to conduct maintenance, and to let their crewmen ashore after many months at sea. The raider *Komet* used Kerguelen for these purposes in February 1941, followed by the *Pinguin* in March 1941. Indeed, the deserted island proved so useful that the SKL considered establishing a permanent secret base either there or on Tristan da Cunha in the South Atlantic, to support both *Hilfskreuzer* and U-boat operations.

Leatham's intelligence staff in Colombo was aware of the Kriegsmarine's interest in remote anchorages such as Kerguelen and occasionally decided to send cruisers to look for signs of enemy activity. Thus, the cruiser HMS *Neptune* inspected Kerguelen in October 1940 – two months before the *Atlantis* arrived – and HMS *Australia* returned in November 1941. These annual reconnaissance missions, however, were too infrequent to catch the wily German raiders. Amazingly, it was not until 1942, when the *Hilfskreuzer* threat had begun to abate, that the Royal Navy decided to mine some of these remote anchorages and to leave a radio-equipped coast-watcher behind. If Leatham's staff had demonstrated this ingenuity in late 1940, several of the *Hilfskreuzer* might have been eliminated rather easily when they were immobilized.

Nevertheless, Leatham used his cruisers aggressively to patrol the shipping lanes around the Seychelles and the Maldives, and they came close to catching the *Atlantis* in late January 1941. Rogge attacked the freighter *Mandasor* 300 miles east of the Seychelles, but the vessel was able to send a QQQ signal before it sank. Leatham responded by forming four available cruisers into Force V to hunt for the raider. Closest was HMAS *Sydney* at Malé Atoll, 900 miles from the sinking, and she got underway at 27 knots. Yet Leatham had no long-range reconnaissance aircraft available to support Force V, and despite the rapid British reaction the *Atlantis* escaped the dragnet. This episode highlighted the need for a Royal Navy presence in the Maldives and Seychelles to support anti-raider operations, and Leatham positioned a naval oiler at Addu to refuel cruisers operating this far south. In August 1941, Leatham's successor, Vice-Admiral Sir Geoffrey Arbuthnot, began construction of a secret air and naval base on Addu that could support long-range PBY flying boats and fleet refueling. By late 1941, the East Indies Command had greatly extended its patrol areas over the Indian Ocean, making it harder for raiders to operate safely near shipping routes.

PINGUIN VS. HMS *CORNWALL*, MAY 8, 1941

After rendezvousing with *Atlantis*, the *Pinguin* went south to the Antarctic and on January 14, 1941, Krüder managed to capture the bulk of the Norwegian whaling fleet. He then returned to the Indian Ocean, but spent most of the winter months conducting re-supply meetings and maintenance. In spring 1941, Krüder resumed commerce raiding operations, but found slim pickings due to the British re-directing shipping closer to shore, where it was easier to protect. After weeks of fruitless searching, he headed north toward the Horn of Africa, even though this was close to the British base at Aden. On April 27, 1941, *Pinguin* pursued and sank the British freighter *Clan Buchanan*. Although the British ship sent out a QQQ signal before German gunfire smashed its radio, Krüder believed that it was too weak to have been heard at Aden. Rather than fleeing the scene of the sinking, Krüder then proceeded further north toward the Persian Gulf in search of British tankers. Vice-Admiral Leatham's staff in Colombo, however, had received the signal and directed the cruisers HMNZ *Leander*, HMS *Cornwall*, and HMS *Hawkins* and the aircraft carrier HMS *Hermes* to search for the raider. After evading British cruisers for nearly a year, Krüder made the mistake of under-estimating his opponents.

On the morning of May 7, *Pinguin* intercepted a small British tanker, the *British Emperor*, near the entrance to the Persian Gulf. Despite German shellfire, the plucky merchant skipper was able to send out a lengthy RRR report with an accurate description of *Pinguin*. Krüder was only able to sink the tanker with great difficulty, and he was now aware that the Royal Navy knew his location. About 500 miles south

OVERLEAF
After eleven months at sea, Kapitan zur See Ernst-Felix Krüder's raider *Pinguin* was finally intercepted by the British cruiser HMS *Cornwall* in the Indian Ocean on the morning of May 8, 1941. When Cornwall apeared on the horizon at 1607hrs, approaching at 28 knots, Krüder turned away but decided to maintain his disguise as the Norwegian freighter *Tamerlane*. Captain Percival Manwaring on the bridge of *Cornwall* signalled for the fleeing vessel to stop but when it did not, he was unsure if he was dealing with an enemy vessel or Norwegians who were ignorant of proper signalling procedures. *Cornwall* gradually closed upon *Pinguin* and Krüder bided his time. When Manwaring finally signalled "Heave to or I fire," *Cornwall* was within 10,500 yards of *Pinguin* and Krüder decided to show his raider's 'war face.' At 1714hrs, *Pinguin* made a hard turn to port and dropped its disguise. As the Kriegsmarine war flag went up the mast, *Pinguin* fired a four-gun salvo. Firing four salvoes per minute, the German 15cm gunners were able to straddle *Cornwall* and one hit temporarily knocked out its steering. Adding to Manwaring's discomfit, *Cornwall* suffered an electrical failure which knocked out his main battery. Under heavy fire, *Cornwall* turned away until it could affect repairs. This scene shows the opening moments of the 11-minute action, with *Pinguin*'s 15cm guns straddling *Cornwall*.

of the sinking, Captain Percival Manwaring's *Cornwall* heard the RRR report, and although low on fuel, headed northward at 25 knots. Unaware from which direction the enemy might be approaching, Krüder headed south – right toward the approaching *Cornwall*.

Around 0300hrs the next morning, the sharp-eyed watch officer on *Pinguin* spotted the approaching British cruiser before the British spotted *Pinguin*. Krüder carefully altered course to the west and the British cruiser soon dropped out of sight. Yet Manwaring followed the book and launched both his Walrus seaplanes by 0700hrs to search for the raider. At 0707hrs, one of the aircraft spotted the *Pinguin*, which was disguised as the Norwegian freighter *Tamerlane*. Unfortunately, Manwaring had instructed the pilot to maintain radio silence in order to avoid alerting German DF teams on the raider, but this only served to prevent the pilot from relaying his sighting report until he returned to *Cornwall*. By 0825, Manwaring was aware of the supposed Norwegian vessel 65 miles west of his ship, but foolishly decided to wait until his second Walrus returned from patrol. Two more hours were wasted due to Manwaring's ridiculous obsession with radio silence and *Cornwall* did not proceed toward the *Pinguin* until almost noon.

Manwaring suspected the unidentified vessel could be the German raider, since no other ships were in the vicinity, but he was plagued by doubt and indecision. While he was trying to decide what to do, the *Pinguin* was unobserved for more than three hours and slowly crept away at 13 knots. Finally, Manwaring launched his Walrus at 1345hrs and instructed the pilot to overfly the target and positively identify it this time – Manwaring would not close on the target until he had more information. Soon, the Walrus was back over *Pinguin* and it used a blinker light to request the ship's identity. Krüder maintained his disguise and even signaled the correct ID letters for the Norwegian *Tamerlane* to the Walrus. After flying around the ship for a while and photographing the target, the Walrus finally returned to *Cornwall* at 1223 and reported about the *Tamerlane*. The photographs seemed to match those of the *Tamerlane* in the Talbot-Booth shipping register and the identification signal was correct, but the *Tamerlane* was not on the list of merchant ships known to be operating in this area. Manwaring could have checked with the naval staff in Colombo to help confirm the ship's identity, but he still refused to break radio silence. After nearly eight

BELOW LEFT
HMS *Cornwall* firing back at the *Pinguin*. Despite a myriad of defects that handicapped it initially, the British cruiser's 8in guns and superior fire control decided the action. (Author's Collection)

BELOW RIGHT
The last rounds from the *Pinguin* are falling short of *Cornwall*, just as the raider is blowing up in the distance. (Author's Collection)

hours of dawdling, Manwaring finally increased speed to 29 knots and moved to intercept the suspicious vessel. At 1607hrs, *Cornwall* sighted the supposed *Tamerlane*. Aboard *Pinguin*, Krüder decided to turn away from the oncoming British cruiser, but to maintain his disguise.

At 1630hrs, the *Pinguin* began sending a QQQ report on a captured British radio, claming that an unknown warship was pursuing it. Although *Cornwall* signalled for the *Pinguin* to stop, and clearly identified itself as a British cruiser, Manwaring still believed that he might be dealing with some very stupid Norwegian merchant sailors. Nearly 50 minutes in silent pursuit went by, with *Cornwall* steadily gaining on *Pinguin*, until Manwaring finally decided to fire a single warning shot at a distance of 19,000 yards and to signal "Heave to or I fire." Krüder ignored *Cornwall* and continued on, playing for time. Fourteen minutes went by and the distance dropped to 12,000 yards when Manwaring fired a second warning shot.

Krüder realized that he was out of time and that the British cruiser would open fire at any moment, but also that the cruiser had come imprudently within range of *Pinguin*'s guns. At 0715hrs, *Pinguin* turned to port and unmasked its guns and Kriegsmarine colors. Amazingly, the opening salvo at a range of 10,500 yards straddled *Cornwall*. Just as the action was commencing, the *Cornwall*'s main battery, operating in centralized director control mode, was disabled for seven minutes by an electrical circuit failure that left the turrets pointing in the wrong direction. Even worse, a 15cm round hit *Cornwall* and briefly knocked out the steering gear. For three minutes, *Pinguin* was able to engage *Cornwall* without any return fire, which forced Manwaring to turn away to open the distance. The gunners in *Cornwall*'s A and B turrets, however, reverted to local control and after manually traversing the turrets, began to fire back at the raider.

While *Cornwall* was disabled, *Pinguin* fired two torpedoes at the cruiser, but both missed. Suddenly, a four-round salvo of 8in shells from the *Cornwall* struck the *Pinguin* at 0726hrs, deciding the battle. One round destroyed the two forward 15cm guns, another obliterated Krüder and the entire bridge crew, and a third destroyed the engine room. Yet it was the fourth round that penetrated the aft cargo hold and detonated 130 mines, which ended *Pinguin*'s career. The raider was broken in two by the massive explosion and sank within seconds, taking with her 342 crew members and 203 British prisoners held below decks. Inexplicably, just as *Cornwall* was winning the action, its electrical power system failed completely and left the ship immobilized for nearly three hours. Eventually, the *Cornwall* rescued 60 Germans and 22 British from the floating wreckage.

ABOVE
The *Pinguin* blowing up after a four-round salvo from *Cornwall* detonates its mines. Only 60 of her 401-man crew survived the explosion and were rescued by *Cornwall*. (Author's Collection)

BELOW
A raider firing a broadside in action. At best, a *Hilfskreuzer* could fire only a maximum of three–four guns at a target due to the restricted firing arc of its main battery. The 15cm guns were centrally directed by the gunnery officer, who used a telegraph system to relay ranges from the 3m rangefinder behind the bridge. (NARA)

During the 11-minute action, the *Pinguin* fired 200 rounds and scored two hits, while *Cornwall* fired only 136 rounds but scored four hits. Krüder maintained his disguise as long as possible and hoped that he could either bluff his way past the cruiser or lure it into effective range, which almost happened. On *Cornwall*, it was apparent that neither the captain nor ship was ready for this kind of action. Manwaring spent an inordinate amount of time deciding whether or not to intercept the vessel and he failed to keep the East Indies Command apprised of his actions. Once put to the test, one vital system after another failed on *Cornwall*, which could have cost her dearly. If Manwaring had been up against the expert gunners on *Thor*, the *Cornwall's* bridge and fire control would probably have been obliterated in these opening seven minutes. Nor was the Admiralty impressed with Manwaring's performance, and even though he was the first cruiser captain to intercept and destroy a *Hilfskreuzer*, he received no decoration for sinking *Pinguin*. Furthermore, after *Cornwall* was sunk by the Japanese in 1942, he received no further sea assignments or promotions. After this close call, the Admiralty advised cruiser captains to keep their distance when approaching suspected raiders and to use their floatplane to the maximum extent possible.

Interrogation of the *Pinguin's* captured survivors revealed a great deal about raider operations that was previously unknown. Three weeks after the sinking of *Pinguin*, British Naval Intelligence assigned an identifying letter to each of the known seven raiders and disseminated this information to the fleet in Weekly Intelligence Report 64. The report was the first to provide approximate size data and specific recognition features for each raider, as well as the correct pre-war identity of the *Thor*. As the British intelligence picture firmed up, the raiders were transformed from invisible, faceless opponents into identifiable enemy ships that could be destroyed.

THE DUEL IN PACIFIC WATERS, JUNE 1940–OCTOBER 1941

Korvettenkapitän Kurt Weyher's *Orion* was the first *Hilfskreuzer* to operate in the Pacific, in June 1940, followed by Kapitän zur See Robert Eyssen's *Komet* in September. Unlike the Indian Ocean or South Atlantic, Commonwealth naval forces in the Pacific were not under a single area command, but consisted of the Royal Navy's China Station, the Royal Australian Navy and the Royal New Zealand Navy. Furthermore, German raiders operating in the Pacific were able to obtain some covert logistical support from the Japanese, and British warships could not pursue them freely into Japanese waters. While the Australians and New Zealanders kept their cruisers close to their main ports to protect coastal commerce, the three cruisers of the British 5th Cruiser Squadron in Singapore spent most of their time guarding the vital Strait of Malacca.

Between June and December 1940, *Orion* and *Komet* worked together to eliminate 18 ships totaling 127,000 tons, and Eyssen dubbed them the Kriegsmarine's "Far

Orion on the prowl in heavy seas. Even when relatively close, the *Hilfskreuzer* were tough to spot and they became very adept at sneaking up on their opponents. (NARA)

Eastern Squadron." On the night of June 13/14, Weyher boldly entered the Hauraki Gulf off Auckland and began laying 228 mines within sight of the Culver lighthouse, which was operational. Incredibly, during the seven-hour minelaying operation *Orion*'s crewmen saw the cruiser HMNZ *Achilles* and the AMC HMS *Hector*, as well as four other freighters, pass nearby to enter Auckland. *Orion*'s minelaying went completely unnoticed and the Germans were astounded by the lax attitude toward security around New Zealand.

The closest the British came to catching either one of these raiders occurred two months later, when *Orion* attacked the *Turakina* off the New Zealand coast and the freighter sent off a detailed QQQ report before it was overwhelmed. The cruisers HMNZ *Achilles* and HMAS *Perth* were quickly dispatched toward the scene of the sinking and air patrols were organized to search for the raider. Weyher beat a hasty retreat, but before he could clear the area, the *Orion* – disguised as a Dutch freighter – was overflown by a RNZAF Vickers Vildebeest bomber. Yet as so often happened, aerial reconnaissance accepted the raider's disguise as genuine and Weyher made good his escape. A week later, *Orion* was spotted off the coast of Australia by a RAAF Lockheed Hudson, but the aircraft also believed the raider was a Dutch ship. The Germans were amazed to find that the RNZAF broadcast details about its patrol areas over civilian radio, enabling the raiders to avoid most air searches.

The 6in gun crew in action aboard HMS *Orion*. One crew member has just rammed the shell into the breech with a hand rammer, while the sailor in the foreground is taking the cordite charge from the hoist. (IWM, A 23468)

Both *Komet* and *Orion* were able to utilize remote atolls in the Marshall, Caroline, and Mariana Islands for resupply and maintenance activity, often with the knowledge of Japanese authorities. Three German supply ships routinely sailed from Yokohama to keep the two raiders topped up with food and fuel, while the German naval attaché in Tokyo was allowed to purchase items for them, including a Nakajima 90-11 floatplane for *Orion*. Unlike raider captains operating in the Atlantic and Indian Ocean, Eyssen had difficulty unloading his prisoners since the supply ships supporting him did not often return to Europe, and Japan could not accept prisoners since it was still

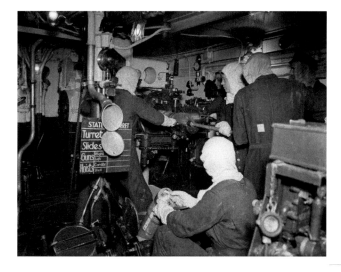

neutral at this time. As the prisoners kept piling up, draining his shipboard resources, Eyssen decided to drop off 500 of them on the remote Emirau Island four days before Christmas 1940. This proved to be a poor decision, since the prisoners were soon rescued by Commonwealth forces and they revealed that German raiders were operating disguised as Japanese freighters and using Japanese-held islands. Due to Eyssen's haste to dispose of prisoners, British intelligence gained a windfall about German raider operations in the Pacific.

Adding to this indiscretion, Eyysen decided to bombard the phosphate production facility at Nauru Island without prior approval from the SKL on 27 December 1940. This attack, which had no real miltary value, energized the Commonwealth forces in Asia to take more active measures against the raiders, particularly in the area of sharing information about merchant ship movements and operational security. Aware that the war was now intruding into their coastal waters, the RAAF and RNZAF began serious air patrols to make commerce-raiding more hazardous, at least around major ports. Using the information gained from Eyssen's released captives, the Admiralty re-routed merchant traffic away from the areas where the raiders were operating and the amount of sinkings dropped off sharply. Thereafter, *Komet* and *Orion* sank only three more ships in the next eight months before returning safely to Europe by the end of 1941.

KORMORAN VS. HMAS *SYDNEY*, NOVEMBER 19, 1941

Korvettenkapitän Theodor Detmers' *Kormoran* was the last of the original seven *Hilfskreuzer* to sail, and it did not reach its operational area between Brazil and Africa until January 1941. In three months, Detmers eliminated eight British merchant ships and then shifted to the Indian Ocean, where he sank three more during June–September 1941. The *Kormoran* had a number of close calls in both the South Atlantic and Indian Ocean, where British cruisers responded to RRR signals. In the Bay of Bengal, *Kormoran* was spotted and pursued by HMS *Canton,* which was a very fast and powerful AMC armed with nine 6in guns and, unusually, a floatplane. Unlike Kähler on *Thor*, Detmers decided not to try his gunnery against the *Canton*, a judgment which was prudent, since the light cruiser HMS *Durban* was also in the vicinity. Somehow, Detmers managed to shake the *Canton* and escaped back into the deep blue.

By the summer of 1941, the situation had begun to change in the Indian Ocean. British merchant ships stuck closer to shore, where they could receive some protection from RAF patrol aircraft, while the *Hilfskreuzer* became increasingly reluctant to risk operating close to shore after the loss of the *Pinguin*. Detmers spent weeks cruising

Kormoran, taken during a supply rendezvous with a U-boat in March 1941. Detmers took eight enemy merchantmen in his first three months operating in the Atlantic, but by the time that he moved to the Indian Ocean in mid 1941, pickings were slim. (Bundesarchiv, Bild 146-1969-117-48, Fotograf: Winkelmann)

around the central Indian Ocean without sighting anything, and sank his last Allied freighter on September 26. He then proceeded eastward to rendezvous with the supply ship *Kulmerland* off southwest Australia's Cape Leewin in mid October. After refueling, Detmers hoped to lay his 420 contact mines off Perth, but the SKL warned him that a cruiser-escorted convoy was leaving that port soon, so he decided to linger near Shark Bay to the north. Once he got rid of his mines, Detmers intended to return to the Indian Ocean for six more months of commerce raiding then head home.

Yet Detmers did not lay his mines, and he was content to loiter off the northwest coast of Australia for several weeks into mid November. Oddly, he did not use his Arado floatplane very often to conduct searches that would have warned him of approaching enemy ships. On the afternoon of November 19, *Kormoran* was steaming languidly northward at 11 knots when lookouts spotted a vessel approaching from the northwest. By the time that Detmers arrived on the bridge about 1600hrs, it was apparent that the oncoming vessel was an enemy cruiser, and Detmers ordered a turn away and speed increase to 14 knots. The approaching ship was the cruiser HMAS *Sydney* under Captain Joseph Burnett, en route back to Fremantle after escorting a troopship to the Sunda Strait. Burnett was aware that a German commerce raider and its supply ship had been detected previously in Australian waters, but he had no specific warning about the *Kormoran*. Y-Service had some indications of German naval signals off the west coast of Australia, but there had been no recent ship losses or raider reports to provide confirmation. Since he did not expect enemy activity in the vicinity, Burnett did not use his Walrus to search the area ahead of *Sydney*.

Burnett had stumbled upon *Kormoran* without using air reconnaissance, but when he saw the unknown freighter turn away and increase speed, he turned to close and inspect the suspicious contact. *Sydney* approached at 18 knots, coming up on *Kormoran's* starboard side. Five minutes later, the searchlight on *Sydney* sent the signal "NNJ," requesting the vessel's secret call sign. Detmers told his signalmen to hoist the flag identifying the ship as the Dutch freighter *Straat Malakka*. Although the suspicious vessel ignored the request for its secret signal, Burnett was probably not unduly alarmed, since Dutch skippers often failed to know their ship's code letters. Unfortunately, Burnett made no effort to radio headquarters in Perth to confirm if the Dutch ship was in this area, or to inform them of the interception of a suspicious vessel. Instead, he continued to bring *Sydney* in closer with his all his turrets pointed at the supposed Dutch ship, but hesitated to take more decisive action, like firing a warning shot across the bow. Instead, *Sydney* continued to close up on *Kormoran* and kept requesting the secret letters for 30 minutes with no reply. Inside *Sydney's* DCT, Lieutenant-Commander Michael Singer trained his telescopes and the ship's main battery at *Kormoran's* bridge area and kept all guns in director control mode. Meanwhile, Detmers prepared his ship for action and quietly informed the crew that they would engage the enemy cruiser once it drew closer. When the *Sydney's*

HMAS *Sydney* in full wartime regalia. After considerable combat in the Mediterranean, *Sydney* returned to six months of quiet escort duty in home waters. (Finding Sydney Foundation)

SYDNEY VS. *KORMORAN*, NOVEMBER 19, 1941

KEY

A 1730hrs: Action begins with *Kormoran* opening fire at range of 1,500 yards

B 1735hrs: *Sydney* turns to south

C 1745hrs: *Kormoran* damaged and slowing down, *Sydney* fires four starboard torpedoes

D 1750hrs: *Sydney* heading south at 5 knots

E 1825hrs: *Kormoran* ceases fire

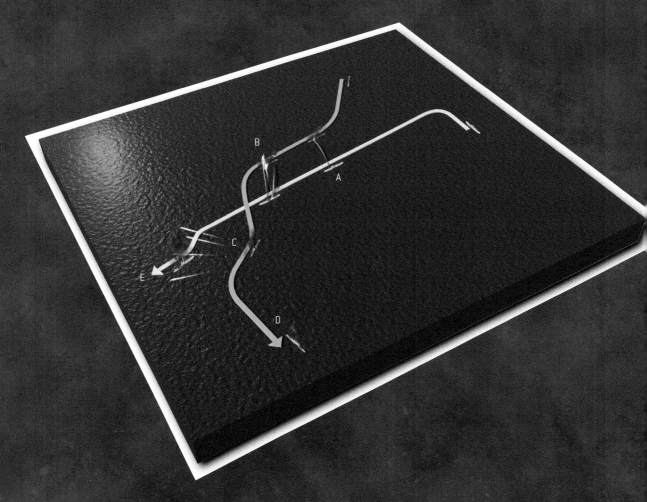

signalmen continued to request more information about the ship's cargo and destination, Detmers ordered the radio room to send out a QQQ signal to further confuse the enemy, which it did. Apparently Burnett was unaware that the *Pinguin* had employed many of these same ruses with *Cornwall* six months before. Finally, at 1725hrs *Sydney* signaled "Hoist your secret call sign."

Burnett appears to have been lulled into a fall sense of security by the clumsy but plausible responses from the supposed Dutch freighter. Although the vessel had acted suspiciously, he had nothing yet to identify it as a German ship and probably believed that if it was an enemy it either would have scuttled itself or opened fire by this point. Burnett apparently decided to make a close inspection before heading back on his way to Perth. Although Detmers denied it later, the *Kormoran* may have actually had the *Straat Malakka*'s secret call sign, but in any event he realized that he could not deceive his enemy for much longer. Yet the tactical situation had drastically shifted in Detmers' favor, as the *Sydney* was steaming about 1,500 yards behind and to the right of *Kormoran*. Although all of *Sydney*'s turrets were pointed at *Kormoran*, Detmers could see that some of her crew had relaxed from action stations and were lining the upper rails, smoking or otherwise inattentive. This duel to the death would be fought on German terms.

At 1730hrs, Detmers ordered "Fallen Tarnung" (drop camouflage): the gun flaps on *Kormoran* came down and the Kriegsmarine war flag went up the mast. Captain Burnett's last thoughts were probably great surprise to realize that this Dutch freighter was actually a German warship, before his bridge was shattered by enemy fire. Initially only the two aft starboard guns could bear on *Sydney*, and one shell from the first two-round salvo struck *Sydney*'s superstructure. Jakob Fend, manning the twin 37mm guns on *Kormoran*'s stern, had a clear line of sight and he pumped about 100 high-explosive rounds directly into *Sydney*'s bridge, killing Burnett and his senior officers. Fend also knocked out the thinly protected DCT, killing or wounding Singer and his fire-control team. Oberleutnant Wilhelm Brinkman brought his two 20mm AA guns into action immediately and swept *Sydney*'s upper decks, killing many of the sailors around the Walrus aircraft, which burst into flames. The 20mm fire also cut down many of the crewmen clustered near the four 4in AA guns and port torpedo tubes, neither of which had any protection. After about 15 seconds of no return fire, someone in the shattered

DCT pushed the pedal firing all four of *Sydney*'s turrets, but since the ship had moved closer to *Kormoran* since Singer's last range estimate, most of the rounds passed over the target. A single round struck *Kormoran*'s funnel and wounded some of the 20mm flak gunners on deck. Then *Sydney*'s guns fell silent for several critical moments, waiting for corrections that did not come from the burning DCT.

In less than a minute, Detmers' starboard gun crews poured six full salvoes – 18 15cm high-explosive rounds – into the *Sydney* at point-blank range, destroying the bridge, the DCT, and the ship's main wireless room. One round scored a direct hit between the gun barrels on *Sydney*'s B-turret. Most of the 15cm rounds were fused for nose detonation and exploded on impact, smashing the superstructure to pieces and starting serious fires. Detmers ordered his torpedoes into action, firing two from his starboard battery. One torpedo hit *Sydney* just forward of A-turret, knocking it out of action, and seriously mangling the bow section.

After a few minutes, *Sydney* was down by the bow, slowing to 5–7 knots and burning uncontrollably. With the bridge crew gone, the remaining crew tried to fight back, but had difficulty shifting to local control and finding the correct range. Normal procedure for local control required an individual turret to fire a single spotting round and then correct, but there simply wasn't time for this method. The crews in X- and

B-turret on the wreck of *Sydney*, discovered in March 2008. A 15cm round from *Kormoran* penetrated the 1in-thick armor plating between the barrels in an amazing display of pinpoint accuracy. (Finding Sydney Foundation)

Sydney's shattered bridge, where Captain Burnett died. The front of the bridge clearly shows large-caliber damage and the DCT has been torn off. (Finding Sydney Foundation)

TOP LEFT
The Director Control Tower (DCT) lies upside down in the debris field on the ocean floor. The sudden loss of director firing at the outset of the action greatly slowed the fire from *Sydney*'s remaining guns. (Finding Sydney Foundation)

TOP RIGHT
Sydney's X-turret, which scored the fatal hits on *Kormoran*'s engine room. The valiant gunners in this turret reverted to local control and were able to remain in action long enough to cripple their opponent. (Finding Sydney Foundation)

MIDDLE
Sydney's portside torpedo launch, with two "fish" still in their trays. The *Sydney* fired a total of six torpedoes but none hit *Kormoran*. (Finding Sydney Foundation)

BOTTOM
A 15cm gun in remarkably good condition on the wreck of the *Kormoran*. Note that the paint was worn off the barrel from heat caused by the high rate of fire. The gunner's primary telescope is still intact. (Finding Sydney Foundation)

Y-turret were further disadvantaged by smoke from *Sydney*'s burning central superstructure. Y-turret managed only three inaccurate salvoes before it too fell silent, but the gunners in X-turret were able to engage *Kormoran* accurately. Two 6in rounds exploded in the raider's engine room, killing most of the engineers and starting a serious fire that drove out any survivors. Within minutes, Detmers lost contact with the engineering spaces and *Kormoran* began to glide to a halt. Another round struck the number three 15cm gun, putting it out of action.

Burning fiercely and down by the bow, someone on *Sydney* turned the cruiser to starboard to open the range and two torpedoes were fired from the port tubes before they were blasted off their mount by a 15cm round. Both torpedoes missed. Even worse, the torpedo hit on *Sydney*'s bow had jammed the gun turrets to port and X- and Y-turret could no longer bear on the target. Meanwhile, *Kormoran*'s gunners continued to pour concentrated fire into their now nearly helpless adversary. With most of its weaponry out of action, *Sydney* turned sharply to port around 1815hrs and crossed behind the drifting *Kormoran*. As it passed at close range, *Sydney* launched four torpedoes from its starboard tubes, but none hit either.

The *Kormoran* continued to fire at the retreating *Sydney* until 1825hrs, but by this point the range was too great and the fires on *Kormoran* were out of control. It was clear that the raider's career was over and that the fire would soon reach the mines stored in the cargo hold, so Detmers began to prepare to scuttle his ship as soon as *Sydney* had disappeared over the horizon. Thirty-six of the *Kormoran*'s sailors had been killed in the action and another 40, mostly wounded, drowned in a carelessly loaded life raft. The rest of the 317 survivors took to their lifeboats and scuttling charges sank the burnt-out *Kormoran* around midnight. These survivors were rescued within a few days by Australian merchantmen and spent the rest of the war as POWs.

One of the torpedo tube flaps still open in its firing position on *Kormoran*. Although it took nearly two minutes for the torpedo to reach *Sydney*, the damage it inflicted was mortal. (Finding Sydney Foundation)

Meanwhile, *Sydney* drifted away, with most of her crew dead or wounded. Perhaps four–five hours after the battle, the mangled bow broke off in heavy seas and the wreck plunged to the sea bottom. Although some crewmen probably survived for some time in the water, none of the 645-man crew was ever seen alive again. This was the largest warship to be lost in action in World War II with no survivors, which provoked post-war controversy about the *Kormoran*'s behavior.

The battle between *Kormoran* and HMAS *Sydney* was the only action where a raider was able to employ its full armament against a British cruiser. Combined with the unusual element of surprise, the firepower caused devastating results. During the 50-minute action, the *Kormoran* fired 500 15cm rounds and scored approximately 86 hits, along with one torpedo hit and numerous smaller-caliber hits. It is not certain how many rounds HMAS *Sydney* fired, but probably no more than about 50 6in shells and six torpedoes. It was a lop-sided engagement that was decided by leadership and quick reactions. There is also little doubt – although unpleasant to Australian sensibilities – that Captain Burnett's decision to get so close to *Kormoran* without being sure of its identity was the major cause of the loss of his ship and crew.

ATLANTIS VS. HMS *DEVONSHIRE*, NOVEMBER 22, 1941

Although the Royal Navy's cruisers found it nearly impossible to find the half-dozen disguised *Hilfskreuzer*, by mid 1941 the Admiralty finally had begun to develop a new indirect strategy for attacking the raiders. Instead of relying on patrolling cruisers being close enough to respond to an RRR signal before a raider could flee the scene of an attack, the Admiralty began to target the Kriegsmarine's support network at sea, which was far easier to find. Tipped off by Y-Service DF about a German weather ship operating near Iceland, the cruiser HMS *Edinburgh* intercepted and captured the supply ship *Muenchen* on May 7, 1941. Aboard the *Muenchen*, British sailors captured the Enigma codes for the *Heimisch* key for June. Using this information, the Royal Navy began to track down and destroy 15 more German support ships in the Atlantic in the next two months, which yielded more information about the logistical arrangements for the *Hilfskreuzer*. By August 1, 1941, the Y-Service was reading *Heimisch* on a daily basis, enabling the Royal Navy to deduce approximately where the

The heavy cruiser HMS *Devonshire* was actively involved in anti-raider operations in the South Atlantic in 1941. It failed to catch the *Kormoran* during a lengthy patrol from January 6 to 29, 1941, but was ordered to intercept the *Atlantis* in November 1941. The *Devonshire* received a Type 285 fire-control radar in May 1941, which it used unsuccessfully against *Atlantis*. (IWM, FL 5884)

raiders were operating and, more importantly, where they might rendezvous with U-boats or supply ships, which continued to broadcast reports using the compromised *Heimisch* cipher.

Yet by the time that Naval Intelligence was in a position to provide effective support for hunting down commerce raiders, the threat from *Hilfskreuzer* had begun to abate. By the fall of 1941, of the original seven *Hilfskreuzer*, one had been sunk (*Pinguin*), three had safely returned home (*Widder*, *Orion*, and *Thor*) and another was en route home (*Komet*). Only two, the *Atlantis* and *Kormoran*, were still active in commerce raiding. Bernard Rogge had hoped to bring *Atlantis* home in the summer of 1941, but the Royal Navy's reaction to the sortie of the battleship *Bismarck* caused him to reconsider. British cruisers intercepted many of *Bismarck*'s supply ships in the central Atlantic, and it was clear that the enemy was on full alert in this region, so Rogge decided to delay his return. Instead, he reversed directions and went back into the Indian Ocean and then the Central Pacific. The pickings were slim, however, and *Atlantis* captured only a single small freighter before heading back into the Indian Ocean.

After more than a year and a half at sea, the *Atlantis* rounded the Cape of Good Hope on October 29, 1941, and re-entered the South Atlantic. British naval activity appeared to have died down and Rogge anticipated reaching a French port before Christmas. Yet due to the loss of so many supply ships in the Atlantic, the SKL ordered Rogge to rendezvous with several U-boats on his return trip in order to refuel them. Rogge was reluctant, but obeyed. He met U-68 south of St Helena on November 13 and then headed to meet U-126 near Ascension Island. By this point, *Atlantis* was suffering from engine problems that reduced its mobility, and its aircraft was no longer operational, reducing its search capabilities. Rogge was eager to get home before the ship's luck ran out.

Using readouts from *Heimisch*, the British Y-Service was aware that U-boats were rendezvousing to refuel with German surface vessels off the coast of Africa, and passed this information to Admiral Algernon Willis' South Atlantic Command. Willis promptly formed Task Force 3 from the cruisers HMS *Dorsetshire* and *Devonshire* to patrol the suspected refueling points. Based upon the intercept of U-126's transmission encoded in *Heimisch*, the Y-Service knew when and where the submarine was going to refuel and at 2004hrs on November 21, Captain Robert Oliver on HMS *Devonshire* was ordered to intercept.

On the morning of November 22, *Atlantis* was stationary, waiting for U-126 northeast of Ascension Island. Just after dawn, she was spotted by a Walrus from *Devonshire*, lurking below the horizon, but *Atlantis*' lookouts failed to detect it. Captain Oliver altered course and headed toward the contact at 26 knots. Rogge was unaware of any British warships in his vicinity, since he had lost his floatplane in an accident the day before and B-Dienst had not intercepted radio traffic from any warships in this area. In due course, U-126 arrived and was brought alongside *Atlantis* to refuel. The chief engineer on *Atlantis* also took this opportunity to begin work on the ailing portside engine, which temporarily reduced the ship's mobility. At this most vulnerable point, at 0816hrs the lookouts on *Atlantis* spotted an approaching enemy ship, shouting "Feindlicher Kreuzer in Sicht!" ("Enemy cruiser in sight!"). U-126 immediately crash-dived, but not before it was sighted by the Walrus, which warned *Devonshire* about the presence of the submarine.

Caught in the open by a British cruiser, Rogge decided to maintain his disguise as the Greek freighter *Polyphemus* and to play for time in the hope that the submerged U-126 could successfully torpedo the *Devonshire*. He used the standard raider evasion tactics: turn stern-on to the approaching enemy warship, broadcast an RRR report to confuse the enemy, and reply to identification queries with slow, garbled messages. However, the Admiralty had recently altered the raider warning report to "RRRR" and the three-character signal sent by *Atlantis* was out-dated and lacked the ship's secret identification letters. Captain Oliver was far more circumspect about handling the suspicious vessel than Manwaring had been on *Cornwall*, and at 0837hrs he fired two 8in warning shots at *Atlantis* and ordered it to stop. He later said, "My object was to provoke a return fire and so establish her identity without doubt or to induce her to abandon ship in order to avoid bloodshed, particularly as she might have a number of British prisoners on board."

Oliver then re-launched his Walrus, which had returned to refuel, to conduct a close aerial inspection, while he kept his cruiser back beyond 15,000 yards, altering course and speed to frustrate any U-boat attack. The Walrus pilot had been provided with a photo of the *Atlantis* taken surreptitiously by a *Life* magazine photographer seven months earlier during the capture of the freighter *Zamzam*. Although *Atlantis* had altered her appearance since then, the pilot reported to Oliver that the freighter below was probably the same raider. The German signalmen replied that their vessel was the *Polyphemus*, but Oliver radioed Admiral Willis in Freetown to confirm the location of the real Greek freighter. Rogge and his crew watched patiently, hoping for a miracle. After nearly an hour, the naval staff in Freetown reported that the real *Polyphemus* was elsewhere and at 0934hrs Captain Oliver opened fire at a range of 17,500 yards. Leutnant Ulrich Mohr described the opening of the action:

> 0935 and the game was up! A spurt of red and yellow flame jumped across our opponent's turrets. [The gunnery officer said] They'll be here in twenty seconds!
> As *Devonshire*'s first salvo sang round us the sea suddenly sprung into fountains of spray from which steel splinters poured, and above the wailing and crashing of the shells came Rogge's order: Start ship! Full ahead!

At this point, the duel between *Atlantis* and *Devonshire* was effectively over, but Rogge held out the hope that if he did not return fire, the cruiser might think that *Atlantis* was an unarmed supply vessel and move in closer to try to capture it. Rogge

The jig is up. Once the *Atlantis'* disguise was blown, it attempted to lay smoke and flee at high speed. The superior British fire control, however, soon brought in accurate salvoes that smashed the ship, and the crew elected to scuttle. (Author's Collection)

ordered full speed to the south in a desperate effort to escape, but *Devonshire*'s fourth salvo began registering hits on the *Atlantis*. Oliver's gunners expertly used the "ladder" method to bracket and then hit the fleeing target. Although *Devonshire* was at the extreme range of *Atlantis'* 15cm guns and the gunnery officer asked permission to return fire – if only for the sake of honor – Rogge refused. He knew that the cruiser had a better fire-control system, and the lack of armor-piercing rounds made it unlikely that *Atlantis* could achieve anything, even with a lucky hit. Standing and fighting would mean the annihilation of his crew and his intent was to save as many of them as possible. As the British shells continued to come in, battering the *Atlantis'* upper decks, Rogge ordered evasive maneuvers and a smoke screen that briefly threw off the British aim. Captain Oliver tried using his brand-new fire-control radar to direct fire through the smokescreen, but the gun blasts rendered the finicky system inoperative. Yet the Walrus still had *Atlantis* in sight and it offered corrections that soon brought the *Devonshire*'s fire back on target. Mohr continued:

> The British shells hit us again, and the whole ship wilted and trembled. For the first time I had that old sensation known only to those whose ship is under fire – that of the deck recoiling physically from under one's feet; of the wooden planks literally straining in the contraction and expansion of their hurt. Her once trim decks were reduced to a shambles of twisted ventilators, of fallen derricks, and shattered rafters.

Realizing that the end was at hand, Rogge ordered abandon ship and managed to save all but five members of his crew. *Atlantis* was hit at least nine times, but finally sank due to scuttling charges at 1016hrs. Once the brief action was over, Captain Oliver decided not to remain in the area because of the U-boat threat and steamed away, leaving Rogge and his 350 men in the water. After great adventure, Rogge and most of his crew were picked up by German and Italian submarines and returned to France by the New Year.

STATISTICS AND ANALYSIS

The Kriegsmarine's *Hilfskreuzer* proved to be a remarkably cost-effective success. In the course of 20 months between April 1940 and November 1941, the first seven *Hilfskreuzer* sank or captured a total of 97 vessels totaling 658,976 tons. Three vessels – *Atlantis, Orion,* and *Pinguin* – accounted for more than 100,000 tons each. In contrast, the Royal Navy was unable to eliminate any of the *Hilfskreuzer* for over a year, and even when they cornered one they proved remarkably dangerous. There were a total of six naval actions in 1940–41 involving Royal Navy cruisers or AMCs against *Hilfskreuzer,* and the British only won clear-cut victories on two occasions. In comparison, the regular surface units of the Kriegsmarine made a total of seven sorties in 1939–41, which resulted in the loss of 58 merchant vessels totaling 321,236 tons. Only a single surface raider – the *Admiral Scheer* – succeeded in sinking more than 100,000 tons of Allied shipping.

British efforts to hunt down and eliminate the *Hilfskreuzer* were a dismal failure for over a year because the Royal Navy expected that assigning cruisers to patrol shipping lanes would result in successful intercepts. In fact, far too few cruisers were available to patrol adequately a swath of three oceans stretching from the South Atlantic to the Central Pacific. Oftentimes, regional commanders were loath to leave cruisers on patrol duty for weeks on end and preferred to keep them near ports for ease of logistics. It was only when a QQQ signal was received that commanders would dispatch one or more cruisers to search for the raider, which was usually long gone by the time they arrived. Furthermore, coordination between the patrolling cruisers, shore-based maritime patrol aircraft, and intelligence derived from communications intercepts was totally inadequate at the beginning of the war, and did not begin to improve until mid 1941. Nor did the Admiralty immediately appreciate the significance of the German *Etappendienst* logistical network, which enabled the raiders to conduct protracted operations in the Indian Ocean. The tipping point came when the Y-Service began to unravel the *Heimisch* Enigma code, enabling the Royal Navy to begin targeting the Kriegsmarine's supply ships. Adding to the British advantage, the deployment of adequate numbers of long-range maritime patrol aircraft and improved operational security procedures greatly eroded the ability of the *Hilfskreuzer* to operate near the main shipping lanes.

Raiders were more likely to encounter British AMCs for the simple reason that, being converted civilian ships, they looked like victims from a distance and they routinely operated near shipping lanes. Unfortunately, the AMCs should have been used to shadow a raider rather than try to defeat it single-handedly, for which their armament was inadequate. The battle performance of *Thor* versus three AMCs clearly indicates that the converted liners usually had a small speed advantage over German raiders, but their elderly 6in guns and reserve crews could not match German gunnery or ship handling.

British light and heavy cruisers could defeat a *Hilfskreuzer*, but only if they started the engagement on their own terms and maintained the initiative. Of the three cruiser captains who engaged a raider in 1941, Manwaring and Burnett allowed the enemy to set the conditions and put their own ships at great risk. How the captain of a cruiser or *Hilfskreuzer* utilized his floatplane also had great influence on whether an action would occur and on what terms. Most of the German captains were willing to utilize their floatplanes to prevent their ships from being surprised, but their aircraft were usually lost or damaged after many months at sea, which made them more vulnerable.

So who won the duel between the *Hilfskreuzer* and British cruisers in 1940–41? Loss statistics clearly indicate that the Kriegsmarine triumphed, in trading three converted freighters to eliminate 97 merchant ships and two British cruisers. Even though three *Hilfskreuzer* were lost, *Pinguin* was the only raider that suffered significant loss of life, while the crew of *Atlantis* eventually returned to Germany by U-boat and *Kormoran*'s crew sat out the war in Australian POW camps. Furthermore, the *Hilfskreuzer* operations in 1940–41 succeeded in disrupting trade in supposedly quiet waters like the Indian Ocean and forced the Royal Navy to deploy nearly half its available cruisers to protect shipping in areas well away from the main theater of war in Europe. However, the Kriegsmarine proved unable to maintain the operational tempo of distant commerce raiding, and as the original *Hilfskreuzer* either returned home or were sunk, the follow-up operations in 1942–43 were on a far smaller scale. As British countermeasures improved and the number of raiders at sea declined, the *Hilfskreuzer* threat dropped off to nuisance level. Thus, early German tactical and operational success with commerce raiding put significant stress on Great Britain's war effort for a time, but failed to deliver a long-term strategic advantage.

Kormoran's gunners aimed for *Sydney*'s waterline. An incredibly tight shot group of four hits near *Sydney*'s midship section and the catapult. Yet the high-explosive rounds failed to penetrate the 3.5in-thick side armor, indicating that even modest protection could make a difference against the *Hilfskreuzer*'s weapons. (Finding Sydney Foundation)

AFTERMATH

By December 1941, there was not a single *Hilfskreuzer* operational at sea. Despite considerable success with the first seven *Hilfskreuzer* in 1940–41, the Kriegsmarine was sluggish in getting the next wave of raiders to sea, and by the time that they were ready the Royal Navy had finally gained the measure of their opponents. Once the British stationed cruisers with search radars at the narrow Denmark Strait, the raiders could no longer use that route and were forced to transit from German ports to the Atlantic via the English Channel. Even with maximum operational security, the Royal Navy was usually aware when raiders were moving through the English Channel because the Kriegsmarine would provide surface escorts and the Luftwaffe would add air cover – highly unusual to protect what was outwardly a simple freighter.

Nevertheless the *Thor*, refitted and ready for its second cruise, was the first to break out through the English Channel and reached the South Atlantic in January 1942, about eight weeks after *Atlantis* had been sunk. *Thor* was provided with a search radar and it used it to hunt down five ships in the South Atlantic then headed to the Indian Ocean. Between January and September 1942, *Thor* sank or captured ten merchantmen totaling 55,580 tons, before arriving in Japan. While under refit in Yokohama, the vessel was destroyed by the accidental explosion of an adjacent German tanker.

Following *Thor*'s successful breakout, the SKL prepared to send out two new raiders. The *Michel* went first in March 1942 and had a successful 346-day patrol in the South Atlantic and Indian Ocean that claimed 15 more merchantmen totaling 99,000 tons, again before heading to Japan. The *Stier* followed in May 1942 and managed to sink four ships in the South Atlantic before running into the American Liberty Ship *Stephen Hopkins* on September 27, 1942. Previously, merchant ships rarely put up much of a fight against raiders and never with any success, but the crew of the *Stephen Hopkins* refused to surrender when the *Stier* opened fire. Instead, a 30-

Remains of *Sydney*'s lifeboats on the ocean floor. Although it is likely that some of her crew survived the sinking of their ship, the Australians did not begin looking for survivors until five days after the battle, by which time men floating in the water would have perished. As would happen in 1945 with the cruiser USS *Indianapolis*, an obsession with radio silence led to delayed response and heavy loss of life. (Finding Sydney Foundation)

minute gunnery duel ensued that wrecked both ships, and *Stier* was scuttled by its crew. The *Komet* also tried to get back into the fight, but when it tried to run the English Channel in October 1942 it was torpedoed and sunk by British motor torpedo boats (MTBs); there were no survivors.

Although the Royal Navy was seriously distracted by the Japanese attacks in Southeast Asia in December 1941, the Admiralty began to implement measures by mid 1942 that drastically reduced the odds against German *Hilfskreuzer*. Prisoner interrogations of the survivors of *Pinguin* and *Kormoran* revealed a great deal about raider tactics and Y-Service intercepts were used to demolish the Kriegsmarine's covert at-sea logistical network. New security codes were introduced to identify merchant ships and the Checkmate system allowed British cruisers to verify the identity of a suspicious vessel by radio. More and better aircraft, such as the Lockheed Hudson and PBY Catalina improved maritime patrolling and deterred raiders from operating anywhere near shore. Finally, in 1942 the Royal Navy decided to mine the harbor that German raiders had been using at Kerguelen Island and to leave behind a coast-watcher detachment. German raiders were still able to operate in the South Atlantic and Indian Ocean in 1942, but it became harder to find victims and much more difficult to conduct at-sea replenishment. Instead, German raiders began gravitating toward Japanese ports.

By January 1943, the *Michel* was the only raider at sea and it was en route to Japan. The SKL readied the last two raiders, *Coronel* and *Hansa*, for a breakout through the English Channel, but British intelligence detected these preparations. When the *Coronel* tried to run the Channel in February 1943, it was pummeled by shore guns and air attacks and heavily damaged. After the loss of *Komet* and her entire crew four months earlier, the SKL was no longer willing to risk running the British gauntlet. The last raider, the *Michel*, refitted in Japan and made one last foray that sank three ships, but a US submarine sank her in September 1943. All told, the final six *Hilfskreuzer* patrols in 1942–43 eliminated 32 merchant ships totaling 214,000 tons, but four raiders were lost. It is noteworthy that British cruisers played only a supporting role in the final defeat of the German *Hilfskreuzer* threat, because the Royal Navy had moved away from the traditional model of commerce protection provided by roving cruiser patrols to a more sophisticated system based upon the integration of intelligence, operational security, and joint operations between the Royal Navy and the RAF.

After the war, the role of Ultra in defeating the *Hilfskreuzer*'s logistical network was not revealed until the 1980s. A number of *Hilfskreuzer* captains, including Rogge, Detmers, and Eyssen wrote their memoirs, but managed to conceal some details of their ship's operations, partly due to ingrained operational security and partly due to allegations of war crimes. Detmers was particularly singled out, since the loss of HMAS *Sydney* with all hands gave rise to suspicions that the *Kormoran* had finished off Australian survivors in the water. Many people in Australia could not accept that a commerce raider could sink such a powerful warship as the *Sydney* and all sorts of wild speculation was put forth, including that a Japanese submarine had actually dispatched the Australian cruiser. It was not until the wrecks of both the *Kormoran* and the *Sydney* were found off the west coast of Australia in March 2008 that the truth about this duel finally came to light.

FURTHER READING

The following captured German records at the National Archives and Records Administration (NARA) were utilized:

Mobilmachungsplan Marine Sonderanlage, January 1938, T-608, Roll 3

Records of the *Hilfskreuzer Atlantis*, 1940–41, T1022, Rolls 2945, 3130, 3131, and 3162

Records of the *Hilfskreuzer Kormoran*, 1941, T1022, Roll 3052

Records of the *Hilfskreuzer Orion*, 1940–41, T1022, Roll 3134

Records of the *Hilfskreuzer Pinguin*, 1940–41, T1022, Roll 3133–34

Records of the *Hilfskreuzer Thor*, 1940, T1022, Roll 2943

Records of the *Hilfskreuzer Widder*, 1940, T1022, Roll 3047–48

OTHER SOURCES:

C.B. 4051 (28) *Report of Interrogation of Prisoners of War from German Supply Ships*, September 1941, Naval Intelligence Division, N.I.D.2 114/41

Coward, Roger, *Sailors in Cages*, London, Macdonald & Co. (1967)

Eyssen, Robert, *Hilfskreuzer Komet*, Munich, Wilhelm Heyne Verlag (1960)

Mohr, Ulrich, *Phantom Raider*, Bristol, Cerberus Publishing (2003)

Muggenthaler, August Karl, *German Raiders of World War II*, Englewood Cliffs, NJ, Prentice-Hall Inc. (1977)

Olson, Wesley, *Bitter Victory: The Death of HMAS Sydney*, Annapolis, MD, Naval Institute Press (2003)

Schmalenbach, Paul, *German raiders: A history of auxiliary cruisers of the German Navy, 1895–1945*, Annapolis, MD, Naval Institute Press (1979)

Slavick, Joseph P., *The Cruise of the German Raider Atlantis*, Annapolis, MD, Naval Institute Press (2003)

Waters, S.D., *The Royal New Zealand Navy*, Wellington, Historical Publications (1956)

Winton, John, *Ultra at Sea*, New York, William Morrow & Company (1988)

Woodward, David, *The secret raiders: The story of the German armed merchant raiders in the Second World War*, New York, W.W. Norton (1955)

WEB SITES

www.findingsydney.com
An Australian web site with a wealth of photos and information about the battle between *Kormoran* and HMAS *Sydney*. It also has many photos of the wrecks today.

http://www.naval-history.net/index.htm
An excellent British website that provides detailed information on the movements and activities of each Royal Navy cruiser.

INDEX